Engaging, relatable, heart-wrenching, and inspirational! This short story has it all! What a testimony!

As a career law enforcement officer, I was always a believer in the "thin blue line." As Amy shares in her story, the world we see is far different than most people will ever experience. As a defense mechanism, we develop a sub-culture and bond at a deeper level than most co-workers in the civilian world. That bond is what allows us to face the dark side of society day-after-day because we KNOW our brothers and sisters in blue and our leadership will have our back. Until they don't...and our faith is shattered.

Revival takes the reader through an incredible emotional roller coaster ride. The author's firsthand storytelling is engaging and relatable. As the chapters progress and more challenges are thrown at them, you share the heart-wrenching agony felt by Amy and Kris. It's stripped down, raw human emotion and you wonder how much more they can possibly take. And then it gets worse!

The inspirational journey that leads them out of the darkness is the true message in this book. Revival reminds us that even in our darkest hour, there is hope. By returning to their faith, Amy and Kris fought together as spiritual warriors and found new purpose. This incredible testimony is a "must read!"

**Howard J Day – Police Chief, retired soldier,
and fellow spiritual warrior**

ENDORSEMENT

In her vivid way of writing, Amy puts the reader in the midst of her story, walking with her through life's trials and tribulations. She gives the reader a glimpse into the deepest parts of her emotions by baring all and holding nothing back. It is heartwarming and encouraging to see the revelation that came to Amy as she walked through the storms of life, and as she dove into God's Word on a quest to renew her faith.

> *"And they overcame him by the blood of the Lamb*
> *and by the word of their testimony."*
> -Revelation 12:11 NKJV)

Amy makes this scripture come to life as she keeps the reader captivated by her testimony, giving hope to those clinging to their faith who might be crying out to God, confused and angry at Him for their situation. You will not want to put this book down in anticipation of how God will work these trials for His glory. This is a must-read for anyone, no matter where the reader is in their walk with Jesus!

Molly Norton, Pastor's wife, board member
with LearnLiveLaunch, Texas

Truth, justice, and righteousness shall be established in the land. It's stories like these the Lord will use to bring it around. Allow Amy and Kris's traumatic, painful, and even at times, confusing story to inspire you of the reality that God really is in control. The truth shall be told!

John Bell, Author, *Life, Life and More Life, The Power of*
Declaring Life in the Most Challenging of Circumstances

REVIVAL

A Story of Loss, Betrayal, Darkness
and the Journey into Light

AMY JONES NEVILLE

*Philippians
3:13-14*

Amy J Neville

Revival
A Story of Loss, Betrayal, Darkness
and the Journey into Light
Amy Jones Neville

To contact the author: amyjonesneville@gmail.com

Published by

Mary Ethel

Mary Ethel Eckard
Frisco, Texas

Library of Congress Control Number: 2022902067

ISBN (Print): 978-1-7357853-8-7
ISBN (E-book): 978-1-7357853-9-4

Special thanks to Jordana Keel for cover and headshot photography.
Contact Jordana at j.keelphotography@gmail.com

"The light shines in the darkness, and the darkness has not overcome it."

-John 1:5

To God be the glory.

CONTENTS

FOREWORD

*"So David bought the threshing floor and
the oxen for fifty shekels of silver. And David
built there an altar to the Lord, and offered
burnt offerings and peace offerings."*
-2 SAMUEL 24:24-25 (NASB)

My name is David Hilton. My wife, Wendy, and I have been married 37 years. We have three children and seven grandchildren. We are a rodeo and bull riding family who also pastor a church and speak at conferences and events all over the United States.

While traveling and ministering to people at rodeos and bull riding events, we noticed hurting people who, at one time, had a church experience but never a real experience with the presence of God. Moses asked God, "How will people know that You are our God if You don't go *with* us?" As cultural Christians, we have gotten "real good" at doing church *for* God but not *with* God.

In the above scripture, we read about the threshing floor. This was a place of process where wheat was threshed to separate the grain from the chaff. In this cultural Christianity we have created, we often miss or skip over the process of disciple-making and being made into disciples. We miss the depth and understanding of faith because we want to skip the pain it takes to be stretched and multiplied. We ask people to repeat a prayer to be born again, and then we tell them to sit down and wait to go to heaven. Or we expect them to serve in church until they burn out. Then they leave the church more confused, disappointed, and devastated than when they entered, leaving with no answers to the pain and hurt. Some leave offended, knowing there must be more to Christianity. We've seen this play out across the United States. The year 2020 peeled back the layers of the lack of faith in the church culture in America. John Wayne said it best in the movie, *McClintock,* "All show and no stay!"

The fact is, Jesus said, *"Go and make disciples."* He did not say, "Go and make members." Disciples are made, not born. It is a process to become a disciple; that doesn't happen overnight! It's the process of threshing and separating, of removing the chaff and keeping what is useful. It's a painful process and, when Christians are not prepared to expect and walk through the process, we lack depth, understanding, and faith to carry us. We lose hope. And when people lose hope, it becomes a slippery slope to the bottom.

> *"Hope deferred makes the heart sick, but*
> *desire fulfilled is a tree of life."*
> -PROVERBS 13:12 (NASB)

Proverbs 13:12 reminds us that we are all looking for *life*. It's a longing God put within us. Only He can fill that void. But too often, instead of *life*, we find death and adversity.

When Jesus was on the earth, the desperate, outcast, and hurting people interrupted and disrupted the religious meetings because they wanted to see Jesus and get the answers He offered. This caused tension in the hearts of the religious leaders toward Jesus because He was drawn to the hurting rather than the prideful. Jesus refused to allow religious protocol, judgment, or criticism to get in the way of bringing hope, *life,* and healing to the outcasts. He is the same today.

When Wendy and I first met Amy and her husband, Kris, they walked into our revival service looking for hope. We saw a broken woman looking for answers and a man desperate to find an answer for their survival. Survival through the opposite of *life.* Survival through the shadows of betrayal, death, adversity, and disappointment. Amy refused to leave the revival service that night until someone heard her heart's cry for help. Rather than being met with judgment and religious criticism, they found *life.* They found survival, which is what the Gospel is. It is Good News! And they began understanding the ongoing process of being made into disciples.

John the Baptist said,

> *"As for me, I baptize you with water for repentance,*
> *but He who is coming after me is mightier than*
> *I, and I am not fit to remove His sandals; He*
> *will baptize you with the Holy Spirit and fire.*
> *And His winnowing fork is in His hand, and He*
> *will thoroughly clear His threshing floor; and He*

will gather His wheat into the barn, but He will
burn up the chaff with unquenchable fire."
-MATTHEW 3:11-12 (NASB)

This threshing applies to each of us. Why? So people can see what only God can put back together, restoring hope, purpose and faith. Our bodies are His temple that carries the glory of God to bring "*Thy Kingdom come, Thy will be done, on earth, as it is in heaven!*" Our lives become a shining light in darkness when we go through the process, which is an ongoing process for all who will follow Christ.

"For many are called, but few are chosen."
-MATTHEW 22:14 (NASB)

Within the pages of this book, Amy writes with openness, wit, and willingness to reveal her heart. Her background in forensic science accompanies her as she investigates the events and happenings of betrayal, death, and adversity. She shares the answers revealed to her from scripture. Her explanations and writings will inspire hope and make the Bible relevant to those looking for the answer to the longing question, "Where are you, God?" This hope will help those who find themselves on the same doorsteps of powerless, corporate religion disguised as Christianity. This hope assures us that Jesus came to set us free and give us power over an enemy set on stealing, killing, and destroying our lives, regardless of age, race, or religion. And as hard as the devil has fought them, you can bet that many lives will be changed from this book that shines the light into the darkness.

This true story gives a great glimpse of what God is after in all of us: Process! Amy has captured the true essence of what Jesus meant when

He said, *"Go into all the world and make disciples."* Discipleship is no cake walk. It encompasses and deals with hurt, pain, disappointment, betrayal, and confusion from our past. But it's worth it, and it's this process that brings REVIVAL!

David Hilton
Pastor, Dayton Christian Center
Hilton Bull Company

IN THE BEGINNING

It wasn't with loud thunder, or gun fire, or bombs dropping
that I met my monsters.
There was blood, but never screaming, never agony.
There was pain, but it was oh, so silent.
It was clinical.
It was always a calm after the horrible.
It wasn't my horrible to endure, only mine to observe.

There was never time to stop and think about the horrible
and how to feel about it.
It was bad form to feel anything at all about the horrible,
so, it got pushed behind me.
It didn't happen in a flash
but followed silently and grew slowly over many years.

And then there was a loss so profound that the utter quiet of it
woke me to my horrible.
Just a field, just the wind, just pieces of glass and metal.
No explosions, no bodies, no lights, no sirens.
And maybe if there had been, I would have felt more at home
and the horrible wouldn't have taken hold.

That's my trauma.
It was clinical, quiet,
and I never knew it was creeping up behind me,
ready to pounce,
until I turned to look for you.

-Amy Neville

"Blessed are those who mourn."

-Matthew 5:4

PROLOGUE

*"The light shines in the darkness, and
the darkness has not overcome it."*

-JOHN 1:5

Dear Reader,

I decided to call this the prologue rather than the author's note because, let's face it, who reads those? But I need you to read this. I need you to understand a few things before we start this journey together.

You see, I am in the middle of this real story right now. I am writing this book in real time and, before we embark, there are things you need to know. Things that are more a part of the story than just, "Hello, my name is Amy, and this is my first book, and thank you so much for your support, and here's what I have come to find now that my book is published." No, dear Reader, this part of the story is integral in my journey, and it comes with a disclaimer, a warning.

I chose the scripture above because it is my favorite, my mantra, and, while walking this journey, there will be dark, very dark times, and you will need to hold on to it. This is the journey of my life, short as it is right now. A journey into the dark places where faith can't be found. A journey into the psyche of trauma, grief, loss, anger, and betrayal. The light gets dim at times, barely discernible, but it is always there. I am here to show you my heart and soul. There are dark places there, but we will shine the light. So, hold these words close and never forget that the darkness has not overcome the light.

Religion is a tricky thing.
So many ways it can be twisted and used for
purposes other than what was intended.
It can hurt, it can divide, it can destroy a person.

Too often we believe we know exactly who God is and what He wants. And too often we get caught up in our own righteousness and we forget how truly lost we are. Or better yet, too often we dismiss God as a fable.

Have you ever attended a sermon or lecture and you could not connect with the message? So many times throughout my life have I encountered a pastor who talked over my head. A preacher who had more degrees than experience, more knowledge than wisdom. And when you are lost and hurting, nothing despairs you more than to hear a lecture from someone who really has had a charmed life.

Please don't get me wrong, Reader. I am not bitter for other's fortunes (although at times I admit I have had ugly thoughts). But it seems that, a lot of times, it takes someone as dirty as you have ever been to help you get clean. When dealing with spiritual warfare (don't scoff, hang in there with me, you will see), I want someone who is battle-hardened to lead me. How can I trust the words of a clean, perfect person that say I can be saved when they bear no marks of sin? I know everyone sins, but let's be honest. Some of us think we have sinned the most and we are the worst of the worst. Our shame is one of the biggest hindrances when it comes to finding God. Because we feel shame and because we feel we are worse off than anyone else, we hide our hearts and fail to seek out the knowledge and support we need.

This is the reason I have decided to pour out my heart and soul and take you on this journey. I have just started, and it won't take you long to catch up. I am not a preacher, not a pastor, no theologian or philosopher. I am just a working-class mother and wife who has stumbled and clawed and failed in my faith. I want to share my story with you, in layman's terms, with no flourishes of prose or evangelism. I want to share my story of how God proved Himself to be wholly other than I thought. I want to show you the scriptures that helped me, and my simplistic understanding of them.

And no, I'm not so arrogant as to think my story is any more special than the next person. I fought the idea. I always thought about writing a book. A different sort of book. I thought about compiling all my weird crime scene stories or maybe my IVF journey. But I could never follow through; I just didn't have the stamina. However, in the past year, I have had the urge to write this story. I began hearing advertisements for book publishing on the radio. My husband and I listen to the same radio station, so I asked him numerous times if he was hearing the advertisements. He looked at me like I'd sprouted another head and said, "No, who advertises that?" I asked a pastor about it, and he said, "If you really don't want to write the book and you are fighting the idea, then you should go ahead and do it. God likes to call us out of our comfort zones."

So, here I am, outside my comfort zone, inviting you to journey with me. If you are a long-lost traveler and you have the anxiety I did about approaching church and religion and are seeking some glimmer of hope in all this darkness, come with me. I cannot promise you some great revelation or mystical, divine epiphany. I cannot promise you some new understanding or secret that I alone discovered in scripture. But I can promise you a real story of redemption and hope. I can promise you the truth, ugly and raw. I will not hold back, and there will be very dark times and themes, because this is real. However, I have found that, no matter how dark my life has ever been, the light never went out.

This is my story. This could be your story.

This is Revival.

"He will wipe every tear from their eyes."

-Revelation 21:4

PART I

IN THE
BEGINNING

"Nation will rise against nation,
and kingdom against kingdom.
There will be famines and earthquakes
in various places.
All these are the beginning of birth pains."

MATTHEW 24:7-8

HINDSIGHT
IS 2020

The year is 2020. Isn't that an ominous way to start a story? The year of whole continent fires, pandemics, locusts, murderous insects, protests, and civil unrest. The year the whole world lost its mind.

But never mind those things. It was 2020 and June, and in my little world, I was aware of these things. But other than the minor inconvenience of being forced to wear a mask, learning how to navigate Zoom, and hunt down toilet paper, these were just fringe on an already fraying tapestry of my life I was desperately trying to hold together. (I started writing this book in July of 2020, dear Reader, so if I suddenly change from past to present and back again, bear with me. As I said, this is a real time journey).

At the time of this writing, I am 33 years old. I am married with two children, an ever-growing muffin-top, and an ever-increasing realization of how heavy and old I am getting. I have two dogs, three tortoises, a snake, a kitten, a rabbit, a fish, and a soft spot for all things damaged and abandoned.

I was born and raised in Texas and, like most Texans, I have an inordinate amount of pride in that fact. I might venture to say I'm prouder to be Texan than American, but it's a close call. I live in a very small town and work as a teacher for a neighboring small town. My husband is an apprentice electrician. We both are very new to these occupations.

From the outside of our lives looking in, we are the all-American family. We work, we play, we sleep, we repeat. From our Facebook and social media, you would think we have a very ordinary, nothing to complain about, life.

But in the beginning of 2020, we were fighting a battle. We were drowning emotionally, spiritually, financially, and professionally. In the month of June 2020, I felt I was close to a breakdown. No, let me correct that. I was post-breakdown in some weird mire of aftermath; not really living but still breathing. I went through the motions every day and I cried myself to sleep every night. I was not happy, and I felt God had abandoned me. You see, we lost everything. We had no friends, no money, no direction.

Have you ever started telling someone a story and said, "Hang on, let me back up"? This is where I back up.

THE RISE

I wasn't always a miserable pit of despair. I grew up in the same small town where I now teach. We lived on 20 acres in the country. We had, at one time or another, cows, a sheep, horses, mules, and any number of household pets. My parents worked hard and commuted. We spent every other moment together as a family; my daddy, my mama, my sister and me. We grew up on horseback.

My favorite memories are taking trail rides with my daddy and shopping on Black Friday with Mama. Daddy called us "boys," and we worked outside the house as much as we did inside. Every Christmas, I would shop with Mama, and she insisted I do at least one girly thing a year (drill team). She always made sure I held on to a few strands of femininity and encouraged me to be diligent in my schoolwork.

I was the quintessential book nerd. A nervous Nellie who had to be the best and smartest and feared failure like it would be the death of me. I didn't have many friends, another aspect of life for me to anguish and worry over, but I always held on to the hope that when I got out of the small town, I would find my niche.

Throughout my childhood, I watched my daddy struggle with Religion. I say religion with a capital r because until recently, that's how big and organized and daunting it felt. Corporate, if you will.

Daddy worked for a Christian company, and he dragged us to any number of different churches and denominations trying to find his place. He read the Bible cover to cover twice that I know of. He "got right" with God, he fell back, he tried again. Even at times when his faith was a whisper of smoke, he held on to doing the right thing because the other option was too hot for his liking.

His favorite line was from a Ray Wylie Hubbard song, *"Some get spiritual 'cause they see the light, some 'cause they feel the heat."* [1] My husband recently told me that my daddy confessed to him that he never passed up a homeless person or beggar because he figured one of them would be Jesus testing him and he didn't want to fail.

And so, I learned about God and how to be a good Southern Baptist, and I was terrified when Daddy went through his Pentecostal phase. I believed. I didn't "feel" it, but I knew it. I had it in my head, and I did what I should. At twelve years old I told my parents I was ready to be baptized. It seemed the right age and I did believe everything the Bible and church had told me. I didn't "feel" it, but I knew it. And so, it was done.

Leaving Home

I managed to graduate and leave the little hometown. I was valedictorian and gained admission to a well-known Christian university in Texas. I knew I was good at science, and I loved animals. I briefly contemplated becoming a veterinarian, but Texas A&M had a wait list, and I was much too soft-hearted.

I decided to get my bachelor's degree in forensic science, and I minored in both chemistry and biology. It was the 2000s and CSI (Crime Scene Investigation) was all the rage. It seemed like a logical field that would never go out of business. With my head for science and too-soft-spot for animals, and with too much impatience for a doctorate, I dived in.

My parents were supportive, and Mama spent hours researching schools and majors and scholarships to get me there. I studied things like anatomy, forensic chemistry, human remains, osteology, immunology, ballistics, and more. It was exciting and diverse. It was hard. I had a hard time adjusting to bigger city living, but I knew what my parents wanted and expected of me, so I toughed it out. (I wasn't exactly tough about it, though. I contemplated dropping out numerous times and drove the three hours home every other weekend.)

I didn't attend church regularly, but being at a Christian university, I did attend chapel twice a week and took a few courses on Christian studies. It was in college where I found and clung to my favorite scripture, *"The light shines in the darkness, and the darkness has not overcome it."* [2]

I still believed, still checked the right boxes, and tried not to get into too much trouble. I even ventured to an atheist meeting a friend invited me to and tried my hand at explaining why I believed. I didn't understand the difference in believing and feeling.

When you have no feeling and no conviction behind your belief, others will not follow.

But despite that disastrous night of atheist versus Christianity, I held on to, "Well if I'm wrong, I'm wrong, but if I'm right, I'm not burning."

My First Career Move

During my junior and senior college years, I landed a job with the local police department as a dispatcher. I worked part-time in the evenings and got my first dose of reality. I learned a lot and began to realize how treacherous the world can be. Being raised in a sheltered family, I finally caught a glimpse of evil. Twice I had victims die while I was on the phone with witnesses trying to save them or get them help. I was cursed out too many times to count, and I had developed a list of my "regulars," those poor souls who called 911 just to talk to someone. Most of the regulars were crazier than bedbugs, but I had a sense of relief when all they needed was a couple minutes of human connection rather than calling in to report something awful.

Dispatchers are oftentimes the unsung heroes and deal with more than anyone realizes. I gained a sense of pride in my work and in my future career. I believed in the team I was on, and I started to believe in the blue brotherhood. Police in general have adopted blue as their color and, because of the nature of the job, there is a camaraderie akin to military sentiments. It is a feeling of family and the sense you have to trust your colleagues with your life. Only those I worked with truly understood the stress and could relate to the experiences of the job. At one point, I had a boyfriend request that I not bring up anything work-related in front of him or his family, as it was just too dark. For this reason, in this profession, we become close, mostly because the world around us is closed to us. No one truly wants to see, hear, or feel what the police do.

After graduation, I got a job as a crime scene technician for a police department outside Fort Worth, Texas. It was there I learned about life, about death, and about how fickle faith is when the "feeling" is absent.

THE FALL

I wish I could pinpoint the exact event, or circumstance, or moment I lost faith. But I do not think there was a single moment. There was no immediate fallout, no singular catastrophic event (although there have been several throughout my life). It was a gradual crumbling away. A slow erosion. An indiscernible slope downward with a few stumbling steps and a faceplant at the end that left me scratching my head and wondering how I got into such a pit.

Doubt is like an infection. A single, needling doubt breaks the skin and slowly spreads through the blood until the entire body is affected. Or maybe I never really had faith at all. Can it truly be called faith if it is untested and unfeeling? Perhaps not. Perhaps I convinced myself that, as long as my head was on board, the rest would follow and that would be enough.

I had grown up thinking that, after biblical times, God withdrew from His people. He gave us free will and it was up to us to make the most of life. I similarly believed the Devil had much more important things to do holding dominion over hell than getting involved in the affairs of earth. I viewed both God and the Devil as absent rivals who sat back and let us make our own mess or triumph of things, waiting until the day they would greet us at their gates with either a "Well done!" or a "Welcome to Hell!" And although I am just now piecing together the puzzle, believe me when I say, dear Reader, they are present, they are working, and it is a battle for every soul.

As I sit banging out these thoughts, I realize the knowing is only a small portion of true faith. And maybe that is why it was doomed to fail. I had no conviction behind my belief. My belief and my heart were lukewarm. Well, dear Reader, God soon put an end to that. He used my interest in investigation, in problem solving, and in studying the evidence to open my heart and eyes to the truth of who He is, apart from the religion and deceitful thoughts I believed were truth. And He did this in a way that could not be ignored.

In crime scene investigation, we learn there are no coincidences. No connections can be ignored, and every piece of evidence or information is relevant. These make up the roadmap of the crime. To assume something is coincidence is to ignore its value in an investigation. So, why do we ignore coincidences in life? Why do we brush off these events as mere happenstance?

In a world of chaos, do not ignore the signs and always remember: There are no coincidences.

The Introduction into CSI

When I began my career in law enforcement, I had a charmed several months where no one died under suspicious circumstances in my town. The running joke was about "when Amy would get her first signal 27" (deceased person). I didn't really notice it then, but this only served to increase my anxiety. The only dead person I had ever seen was my grandmother, and I was terrified to see her lying in her coffin, waxy and pale, perfectly still. As natural as death is, it was the most unnatural thing I had experienced. That terrifying moment when I looked at my grandmother's face and did not see my grandmother was a revelation. It eventually served me well. Knowing the person on the floor was no longer occupying the body helped me work my scenes.

I got a slow introduction to crime scene investigation by working simple assaults and property crimes, like burglary or vandalism. But death is never far away, and the day finally came for me to see my first dead body.

I was still in training, so my partner and the only other crime scene technician in our unit was with me, as well as a gaggle of officers and detectives who must have been bored. The decedent (deceased person) was an elderly man who lived alone. He had committed suicide. The consensus was that, rather than get sick and die a slow death, he chose to end his life on his own terms.

I was shocked and could not understand how a person could come to this decision. I was also shocked by the difference in seeing pictures and mock scenes and being up close and personal with a corpse. I was nervous but determined to put forth a tough exterior. The detectives could sense my anxiety. As I leaned over the man's body attempting to photograph the gunshot wound, the lead detective nudged the chair, making me think the dead guy moved. When I say I nearly peed my pants, I mean I peed my pants a little. Everyone had a good laugh, and I developed a complex about zombies.

The jokes and kidding helped me distance myself in that moment. But that night, I was overcome with a flood of emotion. I prayed for the man and tried to understand why God would let someone do that to himself. And I worried that in God's absence, a God I believed in, I might feel the same loneliness and despair someday. And I began to doubt.

The Reality of the Job

The day finally came to be released from training and start handling calls on my own. The first week I was charged with being on call overnight, I worked three suicides. Trial by fire. One of these would trigger an inner turmoil I had been shoving to the darkest recesses of my mind for my entire life. I got the call late one night in the fall. I remember it being chilly but not cold. The address was in the apartment complex across the street from my own, so it didn't take long to arrive on scene.

Usually, by the time crime scene arrives, officers have secured the scene and removed unnecessary persons. Family, victims, suspects, and onlookers have typically been removed to a safe distance and CSI's don't have to deal with their questions or emotions. Our job is the scene, and we prefer it that way. This allows us to put the scene in a box. To compartmentalize the job and keep the human aspect of it at bay. It is how we survive mentally. I was still new at learning how to separate my emotions on scene. Being an empathetic person, it is difficult to put up safeguards, but I was getting more accustomed to it.

As I approached the apartment, an officer was leading a distraught woman away from the scene. When we got close, she slipped away from the officer and grabbed me by the shoulders crying. "Why?" she screamed. "Why would he do this to me?" Stunned, I couldn't say a thing. The officer gently directed her away. The sergeant on scene told me the woman was the victim's fiancé. She had brought their one-year-old son over for dinner. She found her fiancé, an Iraq war veteran, in the bathtub with his rifle. The sergeant faced me with a hand on my shoulder and said, "I want to prepare you. This is the worst scene I've ever worked. But I will be with you the whole time, whatever you need."

Within a couple of minutes, my safeguards had been destroyed. I could feel panic welling up in my chest. But always the perfectionist, I put on a brave face and decided failure wasn't an option.

I won't go into too much detail, dear Reader, but I will say that nothing prepared me for the sights and smells and sounds. On paper, in photos, everything is sterile and emotionless. It's our job to document that way so justice is objective. However, being in the scene is not that way.

I was greeted by a sharp, metallic odor. Blood. Most investigators will tell you horror stories of decomposition and the awful smell of a body left to rot. It is the smell we associate with death, and it can be vomit-inducing. (I can proudly say that I have never vomited on a scene, although I have come close while pregnant.) I think blood is worse. Decomposition is heavy and awful but somehow familiar. We've all smelled a dead mouse or rotting food. Blood, however; blood has emotion in it.

**Blood signals something very wrong has happened.
It is sharp, and angry, and permeating, and distinct.
It is a smell I dread to this day.**

I hadn't gone far into the apartment when I noticed a pinkish, yellow piece of skull in the living room floor. I was slightly surprised at this revelation, that bones are not the white, bleached version I had studied in college. I pondered at this difference before realizing how out of place this piece of bone was. At the time, I couldn't register what I was seeing, it was so far removed from the bathroom.

The sergeant was true to his word. He held onto my arm as I leaned into the bathroom to survey the scene. I promptly turned and told him I needed to get my equipment. I am forever thankful he gave me time. I sat in my car crying for 15 minutes. I called my mama and told her how much I loved her and Daddy. I cried and again began to wonder, where was God? How could this happen? How could this man who fought for his country come to this hopeless end? I pressed on. And, again, I began to doubt.

More Reality

The most heart wrenching case came on a hot summer day at another apartment. My town was a mass of apartments and neighborhoods. A young man in his twenties had not been heard from in several days. Officers performed a welfare check and found him deceased in an old recliner—another suicide.

The power had been shut off and it was dark and dusty inside. The victim was lying in the recliner, feet up, headphones on, gun in hand. The music had stopped playing. I could tell he had been gone 2-3 days. I was sad we had to be the ones to find him. Strangers in his home, no family. I found a spiral he had written in, a make-shift journal. Back at the police department, I made the mistake of reading it. He had been depressed for a long time and the notebook was a record of all the things he had tried. Therapy, self-help books, doctors, diets, fasts, and finally, he said he prayed. His last entry broke my heart. I knew the ending. And my doubt grew.

Over the next few years, I saw many more horrors and I became very good at building my defenses. I became bitter and cynical about humanity. It seemed to come with the territory. I also developed symptoms of post-traumatic stress syndrome. I hated to call it that. I felt I had no right. I had never seen combat nor feared for my life. But nevertheless, I had flashbacks of scenes, I had nightmares and trouble sleeping, and I had panic attacks for no reason. I went to doctors, I got medicated, I saw a counselor, and I pressed on.

And despite my doubt, I still hung onto the belief that God was up there, somewhere, and I just had to keep on keeping on and, someday He would explain it all to me. I believed it, but I felt a deep and profound sadness that He would not speak to me. And even though my doubt blotted out my faith, I kept going through the motions.

A REPRIEVE

During this time, I went through a nasty breakup with my fiancé, whom I dated all through college. He failed to remain faithful, and I was devastated. Like most young people, I figured I was meant to be alone because there was no way I could convince another guy to love me. I did manage to snag a guy for eight months, but he decided to end things as well.

Between the heartbreak and the job, I was a mess. I began having health issues. I was diagnosed with endometriosis and had two surgeries within a period of six months. And, despite thinking God was an absent father, I can see now how He was working things out. Coincidences that can't be ignored. What did I say earlier in the book? Oh yes …

There are no coincidences.

I was sitting at home recovering from the last surgery when God decided to show me the first sign. A sign that, until now, I didn't credit to Him. I was just happy I had found someone, and I wouldn't have to be alone, as my young melodramatic heart had lamented for so long.

It's time you heard Kris's story.

Kristopher Neville was born on an army base in Germany. His parents divorced while he was young and there were many years he did not often get to see his father. He had a rocky childhood and, by the end of high school, he moved out and into his then girlfriend's parent's house. Marriage and two babies followed, he graduated from the police academy, and then divorce hit. All before the age of 27.

The divorce was ugly and took three years. Because of mutual hurts and his ever-changing, impossible police shift, visitations stopped. By the final divorce and custody hearing, he had not seen his babies in over a year. He was pressured to sign his rights away, something he never did, but he did finally agree upon no visitation. He would still pay child support and be privy to knowledge about the two young boys, but he would not get to see them.

Try not to judge, Reader. Rather imagine working 50-60-70 hours a week, not seeing your children, and trying to keep on top of mounting debt and stress. Because Kris is a private person, he internalized most of what was happening with his divorce.

Meanwhile, a band-aid relationship he had started with a dispatcher was in tatters. She had cheated with another officer; an officer Kris had been close to. Kris began to get ill. The stress of a divorce, police work, losing his boys, and a broken heart quickly stole what little weight he had. And that stubbornness against talking to anyone about anything personal began to wear on him. The rumor mill churned that he was a deadbeat dad, a lazy cop who had no energy and was barely functioning, and still, he did nothing to defend himself.

For months, he wasted away. The rumors soon turned into terminal illness whispers. He'd lost so much weight that everyone began to think he had cancer. Finally, while on duty, he landed himself in the hospital with a migraine with tunnel vision. From there, he sought out more doctors and was diagnosed with ulcerative colitis.

It was this diagnosis that led to a comment on Facebook. Barely Facebook friends, just acquaintances from my time working in dispatch, Kris saw that I was having abdominal surgery and inquired, thinking maybe he had found someone also struggling with his disease. I'm not sure how horrified he was when I, being an open book, began describing endometriosis and cystic ovaries in detail. But he stuck around. We talked often and one day we began dating. Within six months we were planning a wedding, and a year after that, we were married.

TRIALS AND TRIBULATIONS

The First Real Test

The first real test of our marriage came after 2 ½ years when it was confirmed I would not be able to conceive on my own. I was diagnosed with endometriosis and cystic ovaries when I was 22. I had four surgeries before we were married.

We began discussing our options. On the one hand I thought maybe we should pool our resources and try to take Kris's ex-wife back to court for visitation privileges with his two sons. We reached out once and thought perhaps we were on our way to reaching an agreement. The plan was we would start with therapy, then supervised visits, then visitation. Kris did not like the idea of having to jump through all these hoops when he had done nothing wrong, but he desperately wanted to see his boys, so he agreed. But his ex-wife had a change of heart.

We made an appointment with a father's rights attorney and took the divorce decree to see about our options. It didn't look good. The divorce decree was ironclad and included a difficult-to-get-around clause about seeking amendments. We were told we needed $20K to invest in the types of lawyers we needed to see it through. I was astounded it would be so convoluted and, at the end, Kris still might not get to see his kids. He began to have ulcerative colitis flare-ups and I worried about his health.

We decided to look into IVF (Invitro Fertilization). I was told by my doctor that pregnancy cures most endometriosis. We scheduled a visit with a specialist. We were told we would need to invest about $20K for all the procedures, medications, and tests. We were offered a loan. I asked about the chances of getting pregnant. The doctor said, in cases like mine, he had a 95 percent success rate which was the best in the business. But somewhere in the back of my mind, I began to wonder if God didn't want me to be a mother. I began to feel cheated. Why give me the desire but not the ability? I was torn.

Now, I cannot speak for anyone else, and it may seem inconceivable to some that we would even consider not trying to regain visitation with Kris's boys. But remember, Reader: He had already been alienated from them for three years. They were taken care of through his child support and insurance, and he also paid half of their medical and dental bills. And I had the chance for a cure with a 95 percent chance we could start our own family. Also, we were being offered a loan to cover the costs. We had no option of a loan to cover the legal battle it would take. As heartbreaking as it was, and as much as it still hurts our hearts, yes, even mine, we went with IVF.

For as much a miracle as IVF is, it is a terrible process. For about a year we endured tests and procedures. We spent thousands on medications. I had to give myself daily multiple injections in my stomach, thighs, and back. It had to be precise and precisely on time. This meant, even on shift, I had my meds with me and had to figure out how to give them to myself. We went to the doctor at least once a week, sometimes twice for bloodwork.

The day finally came to harvest my eggs and Kris's ... well, his swimmers. Kris will tell you it was the most awkward experience of his life having to...harvest...in a room at the doctor's office with people outside the door walking up and down the hall. But Reader, nothing is more awkward than being wheeled into a room, heels to heaven, strapped naked to a chair, with the doctor remarking how full your bowels are. Mortifying.

Anyway, I had sixteen eggs. From those we were able to fertilize eleven, and six were healthy, viable embryos at the end of day three. Next came the hard part. We had to make my uterus a home. So, more medications and hormone injections led us on a three-month journey to see if my womb was of baby-housing quality.

After three months, I wasn't responding to the hormones like I should. My lining was barely thick enough, although we did two extra rounds of meds. The doctor asked if we felt comfortable attempting, and at that point, I was so bruised and tired I wasn't sure I could last another month of "lining fluffing." And so, we did. And so, it worked!

Three weeks after the doctor implanted our embryo, we were able to hear the heartbeat. It was oh, so faint, and just a spec inside a bubble on the sonogram, but the most precious and beautiful thing I've ever heard.

The Second Real Test

At this point, we had a great apartment, a great church (even though I was going through the motions), great jobs, and were excited about the future. Maybe God hadn't left me. And then, late one night, three months pregnant, I got the call every police wife dreads. This was the second real test of our marriage; a test that would eventually teach us how to walk through tribulation.

Kris had been in a shooting.

I was working the night shift as a crime scene investigator at a department in north Texas. I had not gotten any calls for service (crime scenes for me to respond to.) My expanding waistline was just beginning to show, and my uniform pants were snug. I was doing paperwork and listening to music, waiting for someone to do something dumb in the city limits, something that needed my CSI skills, when my phone rang. I remember thinking that, if Kris was calling, he must be on his lunch break.

At the time he worked in a Street Crimes Unit 100 miles south of Dallas. He rode with a partner and was proud to have earned the position. All I remember about the unit is how snobby and demanding the officers were on the radio when I worked dispatch. But Kris loved being able to take drugs off the street and make arrests he felt were important. After the rumors and hard few years, he had earned back the respect of being an officer.

"Amy, we've been in a shooting. We're scuffed up, but okay. I can't talk right now. We're going to the station. I love you." I stammered, standing in my cubicle, trying to find the words. But the questions wouldn't form, and he had hung up before I got anywhere. What came next was a blur of pacing the office, texting the other officers in the unit, trying to listen to the police scanner, and trying to keep panic at bay.

I wanted to rush out the door and make the long drive. Another street crimes officer in his unit told me not to go. "There's nothing you can do here; he'll be giving his statement for a while. We'll make sure he gets home safely."

I can't remember anything else about that night. I'm pretty sure the other CSI's covered the calls for me. I only remember making it home about the same time as Kris did the next morning. He looked tired but nothing on the outside betrayed how he felt on the inside. When he recounted the story that first morning, he must have still been in "work-mode." He recounted everything in a flat, even tone, like typing a report. The following is a summary of what happened.

He and his partner pulled over a truck for a minor traffic violation. During the stop, dispatch told them that the driver was on the "wanted persons" list. It was a probation violation which meant, if caught, he would go back to jail. Kris asked the man to step out of his vehicle and told him he was being placed under arrest. I detected the slightest tremor in Kris's voice when he said he fumbled the handcuffs as he tried to place them on the guy's wrist. The suspect spun around and jumped back into his truck.

Kris stepped back and his partner tried to wrestle the suspect out of the truck as he sped off, dragging Kris's partner. Kris drew his weapon and fired four shots into the truck. He didn't remember if he was running or standing still. He watched the truck swerve towards an oncoming car, as if the suspect was attempting to loosen the grip of his partner and throw him away from the truck. He saw his partner fall and thought he had been run over.

Somewhere in the confusion, Kris thought the sound of one or more of his shots were his partner's legs being crushed under the truck. Once hitting the ground, his partner also fired three shots at the vehicle, hearing Kris's shots and believing the suspect was possibly firing at them. His partner, thankfully, only had road burn. The suspect, who was not struck, wrecked the truck and was arrested.

I knew Kris felt responsible, and I tried to be supportive. I didn't fully grasp the feelings he was wrestling with. It wasn't until later that I understood how bad it had spooked him. How terrible he felt that he fumbled the cuffs. Such a simple thing, something I, as a civilian, couldn't wrap my head around. In his mind, he could have gotten his partner killed. In his mind, he was responsible for every road rash, every nightmare, every stress his partner went through that night, all because he took half a second longer to get the cuffs out.

I did worry about the affects the shooting would have on Kris, but I pushed those worries aside. After all, his department didn't even see the need to debrief him. No one died or was seriously injured, so why bother? But, for all these things, I never doubted it was justified. I wholeheartedly believed everything would be okay after the investigation.

Kris was placed on leave for a couple of days and was returned to full duty before the investigation was complete. We thought it a bit odd. Usually, officers are on leave until the investigation is complete, but it only served to bolster our confidence that the shooting was a non-issue.

Then, Internal Affairs (IA) told Kris they were looking at suspending him. He had violated a city policy by firing at a moving vehicle. We were flabbergasted. Kris felt his partner was in danger of being killed. Did that not trump city policy? (Just to clarify, Reader, it is written in the policy that exceptions include fearing for life—something IA must have overlooked.) IA told him he could not reasonably expect that, by shooting the suspect, his partner's life would be saved. How do you respond to that? What would they have him do? Stand there and watch? Kris called his partner and asked what the outcome of his own investigation was. Remember, he fired too. His partner was cleared. IA justified it by saying his partner feared for his life.

We immediately contacted the police union and lined up an attorney. Kris scheduled a meeting with the Police Chief. The way the Chief saw it, he could understand Kris's first two shots, but not the last two. In his office, with the luxury of replay and slowing the video, he figured Kris's partner was out of danger during the last two shots. Mind you, all four shots occurred within a span of less than two seconds.

That week, a commander approached Kris and warned him not to fight his punishment. He was told they were only considering a one-week suspension without pay but fighting it would end his career. Kris strongly felt that, to let this go and allow it to be on his police record, given the climate at the time, would be ill-advised.

So, we proceeded with all the bureaucracy and, eventually, arbitration.

ARBITRATION

Arbitration is sort of like an informal court where a third party hears the case against the officer and against the city and makes a decision based on the evidence. We were put on a list, but it would be another year before we heard anything. Kris was eventually suspended for one day.

A Miracle in the Midst of Turmoil

In the meantime, the stress on my pregnancy caused pre-eclampsia. I was placed on hospital bedrest at six months. Our daughter, Gemma, came at 36 weeks. She was a healthy, happy baby who only spent five hours in NICU (Neonatal Intensive Care Unit) to stabilize her breathing.

A year came and went, and we fell into routine. Because of our schedules, Gemma spent a lot of time with my mama and Daddy. I tried to figure out how we were going to raise a baby while working the night shift. My shift eventually moved to evenings, and we found an in-home babysitter. We were so busy we almost forgot to worry about Kris's arbitration. He was still working in PD, on the streets, and life went back to normal.

One fateful day at work, I was an emotional wreck. I cried about everything. Happy cry, sad cry, mad cry, and ugly cry- all in one day. Someone laughingly said, "Maybe you're pregnant," which only made me cry more, because I was a barren wreck with embryos on ice. Still, when I got home, I pulled out an old pregnancy test stuffed in the back of the cabinet. I sat down, did the deed, and put the stick on the cabinet to wait for the results. I was about to get dressed when I saw it—two pink lines. I was pregnant!

And then, because logic dies when hormones are involved, I cried some more. I was still on the toilet when I called Kris, who did not believe me. I begged him to come home, cried when he couldn't, and then cried that Gemma was only six months old and I was still touting extra weight from her pregnancy and was about to put on more. Eventually the hormones subsided so I could feel the joy of being a mommy and not having to use IVF. God had finally answered my prayers!

Muddy Waters

The time finally came for Kris's arbitration where a decision would be reached about the shooting. Arbitration was a small taste of what we would later experience. Kris's actions, professionalism, and decisions were questioned, and I caught a glimpse of how spiteful his own Administration could be. We found out in mid-May that the arbitrator agreed with Kris and overturned his suspension. We heard the brass were upset. (The brass, dear Reader, refers to the upper echelons of police work. Those in higher positions like commanders and chiefs wear the shiny stars, bars, bangles, etc., on their uniform. A little extra décor for their years, experience, and position.) They had spent a lot of money fighting to keep this one-day suspension. But we were elated.

The first sign of trouble came immediately following the overturned suspension. The police department administration changed the days off for Kris's entire unit. This change interfered with a vacation we had planned, and Kris had to use more vacation time, but we managed it anyway. As a joke, another officer in the unit printed photos of Kris with the caption, "I fought the law, and the law changed my shift." We laughed at it, so naive to think it wouldn't lead to anything.

Before Kris was scheduled to return to work from our vacation, he got a call placing him on administrative leave again. He was accused of choking a suspect on a traffic stop.

The story gets a little muddy. We still aren't sure how the complaint arose. We were told that Kris's sergeant was instructed to watch videos of every traffic stop Kris had been involved in, starting with the most recent and going backwards. We were also told that the supposed "victim" had not filed the complaint. Internal Affairs filed the complaint against its own officer and would be investigating its own complaint. I was terrified. I never thought the police department would resort to retaliation. I believed in the blue brotherhood and in justice and could not understand why this was happening.

The traffic stop in question was initiated by two other officers in street crimes. The suspect was attempting to throw drugs out the window of his car, taking a long time to stop for the officers. When they tried searching him, he became belligerent and would not comply. The officers called for assistance.

When Kris arrived, the officers had managed to cuff the suspect, but he was still belligerent and not allowing them to search him. Kris walked up and placed his hand on the suspect's shoulder, and they exchanged words. I'm not going to lie; they weren't nice words. Words rarely were in police lingo. The suspect turned abruptly toward Kris and attempted to either head-butt or spit on him. Kris immediately reached up under the suspect's jaw and turned his head away from him. He used a pressure point near the mandibular angle. The suspect can be seen on video smiling.

It was over in a couple of seconds; the suspect complied and was arrested. He did not request medical attention; he did not require any attention at the jail, and he never filed a complaint. After Kris was placed on administrative leave, I learned the original two officers were placed on a one-week leave. I reached out to both through social media, checking in and expressing my confusion. One said not to worry, it would all blow over. The other said not to worry, everyone knew Kris didn't choke anyone, and the city was just mad about arbitration.

And so, we didn't worry—too much. Kris contacted his lawyers who assured us everything would be fine. But the weeks turned into months, and we still hadn't heard any news from the police department. Kris lost all off-duty jobs and overtime opportunities.

We began to hear whispers of rumors in the department. Apparently the "victim" wasn't cooperating, but the police department was wholeheartedly pursuing him and trying to make a case.

This victim was a convicted sex offender, and investigators had gone to the address where he was supposed to be registered only to find he didn't live there. Once they tracked down his actual address, he refused to give a statement. Kris's sergeant called often and assured us he believed in Kris and would fight for him.

Because Kris was still on administrative leave, he could not work any of his normal off-duty jobs, like security. He couldn't earn overtime. In the police world, many rely on off-duty work and overtime to make ends meet. Losing that extra income put us in a pickle financially and I did the only thing a lost little girl knows to do. I called Daddy. Kris and I were both embarrassed and ashamed of having to ask for help, but with little Gemma and baby Gage on the way, we had no choice. Daddy offered for us to move into my grandfather's house. My grandfather and grandmother had both passed away within a year of one another and Daddy had not gotten around to dealing with the estate. We would have to help clean it out and spruce it up, but we were welcome to move in and stay for as long as it took to sort ourselves out.

Betrayal and Disbelief

Due to the result of the stress on my pregnancy, I landed back in the hospital on bedrest for pre-eclampsia. I tried to hope and be happy. I sat in the hospital bed, day after day, trying to keep my blood pressure down for the baby. Kris was able to spend a lot of time with me and I was glad for that.

After a few weeks, Kris got a phone call while visiting me in the hospital. He left the room to take the call. When he walked back in, he had tears in his eyes. This man I had never seen cry, not on our wedding day, not when our daughter was born, not when he lost his grandfather, was about to break down. I panicked, not understanding and fearing the worst. "What's wrong?"

"They issued a warrant for my arrest. Assault."

My heart fell to the floor. I couldn't understand this. It made no sense. How? Why? Apparently, the IA investigator had nailed the "victim" down and told him he had two weeks to come in and make a statement or they would drop the investigation against the officer. The "victim" came in on the last day.

Kris arranged to turn himself in. He will tell you this was the worst day of his life. He was cuffed and fingerprinted. He was processed. He got a mugshot. His heart broke that, after more than a decade on the police force, he was the one being arrested. This man who survived losing his children, a nasty divorce, a horrible illness, and who still prided himself in his work, was now a criminal. This man who, without being called in, responded to a plant explosion in West, Texas with no equipment, to help search for people and save lives. This father who resuscitated an unconscious baby after seeing its grandmother run after his patrol car while he cruised his shift. This officer who took drugs and explosives off the streets, who saved lives and wholeheartedly believed in doing good. This man was being disgraced and turned on by the very system he fought to uphold and protect. After all his awards— a commendation life-saving bar, a medal of valor, an officer of the year nomination— this man was being booked into the jail by his coworkers.

I watched him crumble, and I wondered where God was in all this.

We later watched the interview with the "victim." The entire time he questioned why he had been pulled over. He began to frustrate the IA investigator, who eventually pointed to Kris and asked, "But this officer here, he choked you right?" There was a pause, and eventually the victim said, "Yes."

I went into labor early that weekend. Our son, Gage, was born at 36 weeks. He spent three days in NICU. We were thankful it wasn't longer. I was angry that Kris's department would put our baby's life in danger. I was confused at how they could possibly build a case. We still had the support of his squad and his superior officer, but the writing was on the wall, and we were advised to find a criminal attorney.

We met with one of the best attorneys in Texas. I was nervous he would judge Kris or refuse to take the case. The lawyer had done his research and talked to several officers at the department and in neighboring agencies. He believed Kris was being railroaded. He said Kris had a reputation as a good officer. And he said he would defend Kris. Sitting in his office, just days out of the hospital, with a tiny Gage strapped to my chest, I cried. I cried for our position, for Kris's hurt, and for the fact that others believed in him as much as I did.

We still had a few hopes. We got regular phone calls from Kris's superior officer. Late one night he called, and we were grateful. He was thinking about us and said we could probably expect to hear from the department in the next couple of days. He sounded supportive and optimistic that no matter the outcome, Kris would win at trial. The next day, the department sent its decision. It was as we expected. Kris would be fired immediately. What we didn't expect was the recommendation from Kris's superior. The man who called us that night to encourage us was the same man who wrote that Kris had disappointed him and betrayed his trust and the trust of the public. This was the same man who recommended Kris be fired.

I don't think I can accurately describe the feelings of betrayal and disbelief. I would have rather heard the things written on day one than to go months thinking we had their support. We were told not to talk to anyone at the department, but we heard pressure was put on the officers on the call and on Kris's superior. There was talk of the unit being disbanded if they didn't fall in line with what the department wanted. I went with him to clean out his desk and locker. A whole career loaded in the back of our truck and a three-hour drive ahead of us. But we still believed the justice system would prevail.

Kris eventually started looking for work and bounced around trying to find something that would pay enough to keep us afloat. We lost over half our income. My parents were completely supportive, and I loved being close to them for the first time since college. We clung to them and their unwavering support. And we waited for trial.

Trial took forever. We were put on lists for pending court dates and postponed and rescheduled a million times. Eventually the trial was set for that summer. We all planned to be there. My daddy, my mama, me and Kris's family and friends. I figured the show of support and the weak case would clear him. Our lawyers were optimistic, and life limped along as we waited and hoped for vindication that we knew would happen eventually.

Then, without warning, optimism and hope flew out the window, as my world came crashing down around me.

MARCH 4
THE DAY MY WORLD CRUMBLED

I woke up to a banging on my bedroom door.

Remember we moved to my grandfather's house, three hours north. The house is a maze of add-ons and window units, so we couldn't hear anyone at the front or back doors. I could hear several people outside my bedroom, and I tumbled out of bed, rousing Kris as I went.

When I opened the door, my mama, my sister and an aunt and uncle were standing in my hallway. I was scared as I tried to rub the sleep out of my bleary eyes. My sister told me, "Daddy is gone." My sleepy-brained response was, "What do you mean, where?" I then realized everyone was crying. They gave me the short version of what they knew.

My daddy had wrecked his motorcycle about half a mile from the house. He "didn't make it."

I stumbled backwards, not really grasping what was happening. I put on my uniform. I told Kris to get the kids up and we would go. I don't know what I thought would be there or what I could do. I wasn't grasping that he had died. My uniform was on, I was in work-mode. I bossed everyone around and we all piled into our vehicles.

My daddy was my best friend. He knew my heart and I knew his. We listened to the same music. He took me to my first concert, the *Pink Floyd Laser Light Show,* and I took him to see *Roger Waters: The Wall.* We went to concerts, enjoyed trail rides, and even tried out a couple of bars together. I spent every summer and hunting season with him and my Papa (Mama's father).

Daddy couldn't be gone. He was the toughest man I knew. After a hog hunting trip on horseback went sour and he broke all his ribs, I dragged him out of the Red River. After being thrown from a horse into a creek, he walked himself and his horse over a mile back to the house with a broken humerus. Then there was the time he cut his thumb in half on a table saw. He taped it together, unhooked a trailer, and put my fainting mama in the truck before driving himself to the hospital, even pausing to cuss out a trooper who was driving too slowly. (The trooper saw his bloody mess and simply replied, "By all means" to his "Can you get the hell out of the way?") He was invincible. He couldn't be gone.

We drove out to a muddy, plowed corn field about a half mile from my parent's house. The field was a mess of mud and metal. (The cover photo shot for this book was taken on this road. You can see my daddy's final resting place if you look between the space where Kris and I are holding hands.)

And he was gone.

Crime Scene Investigation

I stood there in the mud. I turned around and around, trying to find him or evidence of him. I stood among the pieces of his bike scattered across 50 yards. I could see impacts where the bike flipped. I could see drag marks where they removed the bike. I saw little red flags marking impact marks where the bike came to rest, and I saw two flags marking angry black x's. X's that told me where his body had been.

I took it all in and marched back to the road. I walked up and down that little back highway trying to find anything to indicate why or how. My entire family parked along the road, watching me, upset, and pleading with me to come back to the house. I made them leave me. I told Kris to take everyone back to Mama's and come back to get me once the kids were settled.

I was in work-mode. I was working a scene. I didn't cry. I compartmentalized. I called the trooper who investigated. He told me my daddy had simply left the road and was most probably killed instantly. I asked about his belongings and his bike. The trooper said the bike was taken to a wreck yard but they couldn't find the keys. I marched back out into the mud and searched until I found them. I answered his ridiculous questions about suicidal tendencies. I asked, "Why would a suicidal person reasonably expect that driving off the road and into an empty field would kill them?" He apologized and blamed it on procedure. There were no skid marks, no braking indications, and no blood that I could see. The only reason the wreck was so awful was that the field was about two feet lower than the road. If he had left the roadway at the speed limit, he would have been airborne. A fact further confirmed by the impact marks indicating his bike flipped three times, end over end.

Kris came and picked me up and we went to the wreck yard together. I was in a very weird mood, not grieving, but almost annoyed. The trooper was immaculate in his uniform. The man who was with my daddy as his death was investigated didn't look like he had investigated at all. He didn't even find the keys, for crying out loud. I was covered in mud, head to toe. I know he might have taken a shower and changed. I know he probably did his best. But, in that moment, I dismissed him as being an unworthy investigator. And I began to fuel a deep-set anger that God had done my daddy wrong and then sent an incompetent rookie to investigate his final moments.

As I surveyed Daddy's bike, I hardly recognized it. His beautiful black Honda Goldwing he had lovingly poured over and added to was just a crumpled hunk of metal. The custom flame decals I made for him were covered or twisted, and the only intact part seemed to be the compartment where he kept his pistol. I unlocked it and spitefully asked the trooper if he would let me retrieve it without feeling nervous. Looking back, I feel badly, but in that moment, he was a podunk highway hog that didn't do a good enough job. In that moment, no one could. It pains me to write this now, but Reader, in that moment, even God had failed.

From that point, I was on my own. I entered a permanent work-mode where I was safe. I helped my mama and family plan a funeral, I called the medical examiner and spoke with investigators. I ripped up the stupid little orange flags, got chastised by the Department of Public Safety, and ripped them up again after his funeral. I picked up all the pieces of metal in that farmer's field. Daddy was always so respectful of others' land and livelihoods. He wouldn't have wanted a flat tractor tire on his account. I just knew Daddy would never leave a mess or put someone's livelihood in jeopardy if he could help it. But he couldn't help it, he wasn't there. It was my job. I picked up all his belongings the investigators left behind. Three trash bags full of final moments. I explained the autopsy and tried to minimize the more gruesome aspects for my mama. Aspects and words I knew the true meaning of. Injuries I had seen and recreated over images of my daddy. From that day, he became every accident I had ever come across. And I knew he would be at every accident I would ever work again.

Although it was clear from the autopsy he had suffered a cardiac event just moments before leaving the roadway, and although it was clear from the facts that, if he hadn't been gone before, he was killed instantly upon the first impact, I still questioned everything. Was he scared? Was he in pain? How long did he lie there? In the mud? In the cold? Why was I the last to know? I should have been there. I was sleeping while he lay there alone, broken.

**And with that, blame and guilt
became friends with my anger.**

Days and months kept coming despite my world crumbling. It didn't make sense that the world didn't pause. I decided I would look more seriously into leaving the field of crime scene investigation. It was a job I struggled with for years emotionally, and one I couldn't really understand why God lead me to. Yes, even in this, I blamed Him.

I began to study to get my teaching certificate. All while shouldering more responsibilities at my parents', helping with mowing, horses, maintenance, and while waiting for Kris's trial for the alleged choking incident. A trial my daddy had promised to come to in support of us. The trial came that summer, just a few months after Daddy's death.

The Trial, the Conviction

I could write an entire book on just the trial. How Kris's rights were violated, how we were denied most of our evidence being shown to the jury, how even simple jury instruction that is standard in cases against officers was ignored, how skewed it was. But that is not really the point in all this. You may inevitably do your own research. You may read articles and see pictures. Trust me, Reader, there is a whole video you won't see. A whole book of evidence you'll never hear or see reported.

The real, true point is we watched as every attempt at proving Kris's innocence and justifying his use of force was thwarted. We watched as his two fellow officers on scene, the two who messaged me their support and agreement that Kris had done no wrong, testified against him. One cried for most of his testimony. Those messages were thrown out as hearsay, so the jury only heard how these two officers were shocked at Kris's behavior and had always thought he had done wrong. The real, true point is how we felt completely, utterly lost and abandoned. Betrayed. Destroyed.

Kris was convicted of assault and official oppression.

What came in the months after was a blur of nasty articles and messages, new jobs for us both, a landslide of bills and debt, and a sentencing: 12 months' probation with fees and other add-ons, and the stress of appealing the decision.

Kris bounced around awhile looking for a new job that would provide for our family. He soldiered on, but he fought his own internal battles, stripped of his livelihood, his identity, and his good name.

I became a teacher and started therapy and more medications. I was failing in my new job and failing my family. I was tired and my head ached so badly, it was all I could do to keep it together until Kris came home from work each night, at which point I would go to sleep. Well, not really to sleep, just to bed. I would sit alone in the dark, distract myself with my phone, a book, anything to keep the thoughts and tears at bay. I looked and looked, but I couldn't see God anywhere in any of this.

It may seem overly dramatic, Reader, but there was a span of over a year where I truly believe my soul died.

———————

**I buried my soul in a mound of guilt and anger and grief.
I was a walking bag of bones pretending to live.**

———————

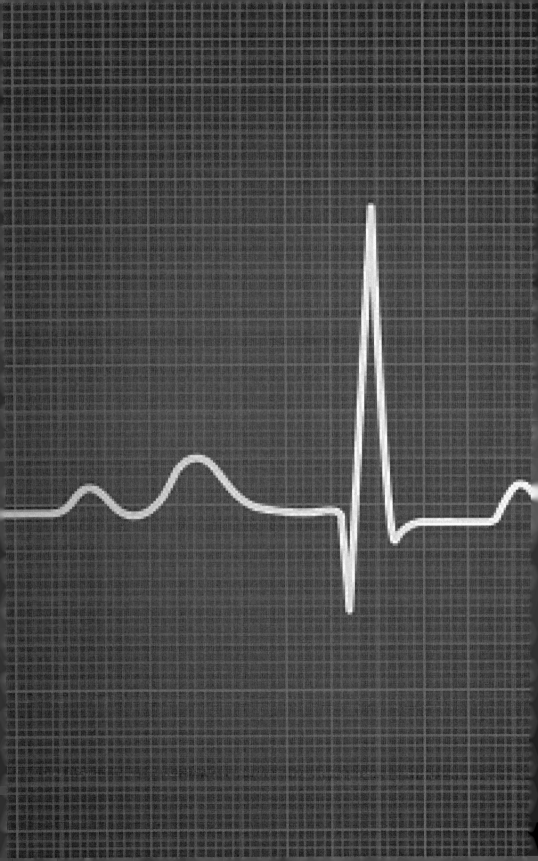

PART II

REVIVAL

*"Though I walk through the midst of
trouble, You will revive me."*

PSALM 138:7 (NKJV)

A NEW CHAPTER

———————— ✤ ————————

And so, we carried on. Not because we were content or satisfied in the way things were, and not even because we were resigned to things. We carried on because there was nothing else to do.

Kris worked a few different jobs before settling as an electrician's apprentice. It was a trade, something he could grow in. Having no degree other than graduating from the Police Academy, it seemed the only option he had at the time.

I struggled with being a teacher. Between holding back grief and devastation and learning a new profession, I didn't realize I was drowning, even though it was beating me about the head. I had severe migraines almost every day. I began seeing a neurologist once a week for injections in the base of my skull, in my shoulders, and up my nose to numb the pain and the intense knots in my muscles. I saw a therapist and a psychiatrist. I took medications to numb the emotional pain. I became a living zombie who could only feel the intense pain of headaches and the nausea brought on by stress. One morning, I had a migraine so intense, I was seeing double and hit a guardrail on the way to work. In my zombie state, I continued to work with a concussion and a dented front fender.

I didn't know how to teach. Yes, I took the classes, but I was thrown into a classroom after attaining an alternative certification. I knew what to teach, but I didn't know how. Pair that with a reluctant mentor and I felt like a complete failure. I didn't know how to ask for help without it adding to this mentor's already poor opinion of me. I didn't know how to not be good at something and give myself time to learn. So, I beat myself up and I sat at rock bottom. I was disconnected from my colleagues, my students, and even my family.

I would get up after a night of nightmares and tossing, too tired to think straight. I would go to work and beat my head against a brick wall of trying not to fail but failing all the while. I would come home and do what I could to hide my feelings and mess from my babies. As soon as Kris would get home, I would lock myself away from my family and the world. Not resting, not sleeping, just existing, alone. I wasn't a wife. I wasn't a mother. I wasn't a teacher. I wasn't me. I was here, but not here. I imagine it was like Purgatory. A bleak place, where there were no more storms, just the memory of ravage. Just the waste. A place barren and hopeless.

A Rare Moment of Fire

That December I flushed all my medications. (Please, dear Reader, don't try this at home.) Looking back, I can't pin down a rhyme or reason to it. I wasn't well. I still struggled everyday with the heavy weight of depression, with flashbacks, nightmares, and panic. Despite the host of medications, there were times when a thought or a vision would needle its way into my mind. They would slip in so easily I wouldn't notice until the thought's repetition would take over and replace every other thought and completely consume and command my full attention. The vision would grow, both in size and in clarity, until I was back in that moment, torn between my present and my past.

But all the same, something compelled me to flush them. Down the toilet went those precious little blue pills and a host of other "mood stabilizers." I had been off and on medication for my entire law enforcement career. My depression escalated after my daddy's accident to the point where, if I wasn't a crying mess on the floor, I was a total zombie in bed, too tired and heavy to move. I found myself taking medication out of habit rather than actual need. Almost as if I anticipated a meltdown. I wasn't straight up abusing my meds, but I left no room to see if I could cope without them either. I was so mindless in taking them, I would find myself chewing them rather than grabbing a glass of water. The bitterness didn't even register.

In a rare moment of fire, I didn't want to be beholden to my medicine anymore. I didn't want anything to dictate my mood. I did it quickly, without telling anyone, lest I lose that fire. Later, Kris worried I might experience bad withdrawals and said he wished I had weaned off. I responded that I didn't think I had the strength to wean, nor the stamina. I had one brief chance and I took it.

My mood didn't magically get better. I was only ever so slightly more awake. By the following May, I was desperate to feel anything other than despair. Those precious little pills screamed to me from their watery death, and I contemplated seeing yet another doctor who I knew would throw prescriptions at me.

Still angry at God, I relented to reaching out to Him, if only half-heartedly.

Reaching Up, Reaching Out

I found a pastor from my youth and sent him a message. I decided my pride was not worth the feeling of utter helplessness, and I had to admit our story to someone in the hopes they could put in a good word to God for us.

I tried to convey how desperate I felt, and I tried to cram the last ten years of tribulation into one message. It hurt to open my heart to someone about these deeply personal things. It hurt my pride to admit weakness. It hurt even more to say PTSD (Post Traumatic Stress Disorder), as I've explained. For all my doubt and half-heartedness, I must have expected a miracle, because the disappointment at his response plunged me back into cold water, and I felt more isolated than ever. I guess I was hoping for some divine enlightenment and a miracle verse to take away years of doubt and pain.

Instead of an epiphany, I got a "I'm very sorry to hear that" and "God will never give you more than you can handle, just go to Him in prayer" kind of response. I was pissed (Lord, forgive me).

Before you hate me, Reader, understand I was at the end of my rope, and all my chickens were in this basket that, if I confessed to a man of God all the trials and tribulations I had been through, he would show me pity and compassion, and God would pour out His divine love, and everything would be rainbows and unicorn farts.

So, when I got a generic response, I was flattened. I was beyond disappointed. Didn't this guy realize I had poured out my soul to him? I told him things I had told no one. How was I supposed to pick myself up and walk into his church when he seemed so casual as to my plight? Again, I am not holding any of my ugly back, Reader. Maybe I hadn't done a good enough job explaining, maybe I was too hurt to read his message clearly. But in my journal my response to this was:

> "So, Brother *****'s message seemed like he had no time for me, but he suggested I start with the book of James. A little confused and maybe pissed off, James seems to be about living right. What's he trying to say? Anyhow, I messaged him again, trying to get more clarity without jumping to conclusions. He'll have to come right out and say he doesn't want to hear from me."

Of course, he never said any such thing, but with his second response, (more along the same lines of trusting God, praying, and studying the Bible), I knew I wouldn't find what I was looking for through correspondence with him. Please, dear Reader, don't blame him. I don't. His response was very appropriately Southern Baptist preacher. It just didn't fill the gaping hole I had allowed to grow in my heart.

(No person on this earth can fill a hole in the heart, Reader. Only Jesus can.)

I stubbornly vowed to try praying. I'm sure those first few prayers were the worst prayers in the history of praying, but I let it all out. I told God how angry I was at Him, and then apologized for it. I told Him He needed to speak to me and apologized I hadn't spoken to Him. I told Him He should have helped us, helped me, saved my daddy, given us a break, and then apologized for being selfish. I told Him this was all I could do, and I needed something, anything to keep going.

Desperate cries, although silent, that I hurled to the ceiling, the sky, until I was drained and left feeling not expectant, but at least purged for a moment.

But things began to happen.

The first clear sign came as a panic attack. I had a screaming, pounding migraine. My blood pressure was through the roof, well over 200/100. I felt like a vise was being tightened around my chest. But in my stubborn pride, I told myself this was not panic, it was just a blood pressure issue. Nevertheless, I landed in the emergency room.

After multiple doses of blood pressure medications that did nothing, a nurse came into my room and sat down. He looked at me and asked if everything was all right at home. I was immediately offended and grew defensive. I was not some abused woman or medicine junky, or any other horrible stereotype I so hatefully harbored in my heart. (I feel shame at this, Reader. After all, wasn't my job for so long to help the very same women and people I was so stringently offended by being classed with?)

He calmly said he felt this was more of an emotional issue than a cardiac one. I slowly began to admit to anxiety, PTSD, and depression. As the words came, the tears came, and then everything spilled out. I cried when I told him how ashamed I was at my weakness, knowing if it had been anyone other than myself, I would have understood this pain, I would have allowed it and validated one's feelings. I told this stranger about my daddy, and my duty, and my expectations of myself to carry the burden of it all. After I ran out of words, he told me about losing his child around the same time as Daddy's accident. He talked about getting through the pain and finding ways to cope. And ever so gently, he suggested God was the only way he had done it. He let a few tears fall and patted my knee. He left and returned with an anxiety medication for my IV. After 30 minutes, my blood pressure lowered, and I was told I could go home. The doctor suggested a therapist; the nurse suggested our meeting was no coincidence.

At home, I broke down, defeated that I was so weak as to let stress send me to the hospital. I raged and cried until my head pounded and my nose was stuffed up.

And with that, the weary calm from all that emotional purging acted like a band-aid to the gaping wounds in my heart.

And as we all tend to do sometimes, I hobbled along with this band-aid, convinced it would hold.

The Band-Aid Fails

Around this same time, mama's daddy, my grandfather, whom my babies call "Little Poppa," was diagnosed with cancer. (He was "Little Poppa" because my babies called my daddy "Big Poppa.") We moved him to Mama's house to take care of him. Three times a week I would go over after work to give Mama a break and him a bath. With Kris working late hours, I was the only one big enough and with the mental fortitude to do it. When I say mental fortitude, I really mean the ability to detach myself from a situation.

After a few months of growing weaker, Little Poppa stood up one night to head to bed, told Mama he couldn't breathe, laid down and passed away in the living room floor. I got the call and drove over 100 mph to get there, but I was too late. All I could do, as I had done, was clean up and help Mama through another devastating loss.

A few days later, with the band-aid soaked through and hanging on with its worn-out adhesive, we were helping my mom feed horses, haul off trash, and other land duties we inherited after Daddy passed. As we left, my zombie-mind stared out the window and noticed baby cows in the pasture across from the homestead. Gemma and Gage were excited, so I asked Kris to pull over and I would see if they would come to the fence.

After a couple of minutes, a petite lady came jetting over on a side-by-side (an all-terrain vehicle). I'm sure she was suspicious of this crazy, worn-out lady staring at the cows in the middle of the country. She was dressed in scrubs and, although she was smaller than me, she carried authority. She introduced herself as Olivia and I explained who I was. She knew my parents and about my daddy's accident. She hadn't heard about Little Poppa yet.

The band-aid fell off and my eyes betrayed me. Tears began to roll, and Kris stepped out of the truck. As we chatted, her husband, Joey, came over. As he approached, I saw his motorcycle vest and was stabbed in the chest with the unfairness of this meeting. Why? I didn't need a reminder of Daddy. So, steeling myself against an onslaught and trying not to embarrass my husband, I tried to act nonchalantly about it all.

They began sharing their own horrific story, every bit, if not more, heart-wrenching than our own. Again, my good old friend, shame, stopped by to add more tears to the pile. Joey mentioned his church where he is a lay pastor. I laughed bitterly and said he was the second person in a week to mention God to me. He just nodded, knowingly, and invited us to attend Revival.

In my mind, I saw a tent and a bunch of holy rollers I had witnessed the time Daddy dragged us to a Pentecostal church on one of his many endeavors to find his perfect church home. As a kid, it mostly scared the Jesus out of, rather than into, me.

Kris, however, seemed eager. He recognized the pastor's name. Back in the truck, Kris reminded me that the pastor had given the invocation at a law enforcement training conference we attended years prior. I vaguely remembered meeting the man but the only thought I could drum up was, (Lord and Pastor forgive me), "Very tall, Amish guy."

The Revival was scheduled to start in three days. I began to prepare my excuses.

REVIVAL

re·vive

/re'vīvl/ verb

restore to life or consciousness

The first day of Revival came. I'm not sure whether I had no good excuses, or I was so tired I couldn't argue when Kris insisted we go. I dug out my journal, convincing myself this show of effort would once and for all prove I had done all I could do, and if God didn't meet me, then I would have my answer. Please be kind, Reader, I know how awful that sounds, but I am laying it bare.

**As if taking a journal under the pretense
of being a good student
can cross the vast distance between sin and righteousness,
between selfishness and true love.**

I didn't write in the journal until after the third nights service, but I did think back and write about my observations for all the nights. To express exactly how I felt in each moment, I am laying out my journal entries during Revival and the Sunday following. Please remember my mental state, Reader. Those huge holes in my heart left a lot of room for bitterness and plenty of ugly thoughts about people.

Night 1

They (Mama's neighbors) brought up God and prayed for us. They invited us to revival at their church. And we came. The first night I didn't get it. I didn't like the speaker. I didn't like the children's church process for the kids. I didn't like the way people worshipped. It was overwhelming and I felt like I didn't belong. But Kris did—and the babies loved it. So, I decided to try again the next night and I asked God to let the speaker "know" about me and give me a sign.

Night 2

I didn't really like the music, but I cried—a lot. I felt a lot, as though my emotions were raw. The speaker was good, and I waited for him to call me out or speak to me, to give me the message I asked for—it didn't happen. I was disappointed and more heartbroken than I thought I could be. Why? Because I told myself all along that God was too busy to bother with my trivial heartache. Kris was in love with the church and the message and inspired, so I swallowed my regret at agreeing to attend, and vowed to see this Revival through, at least for him and the kids.

I wrote a six-page letter that night, using both the front and back of the paper, detailing my hurt, my anger, my loss, our struggles. I told of deeply personal and secret things. I hesitated divulging all. I didn't want pity and I didn't want anyone to judge me or my family. But in the end, I wrote it all, every detail, every bloody and horrible memory, every betrayal, and every loss. I was determined at the very least to give it to the Pastor and hope that maybe I'd get a church call or something later. This was my final show of faith, the only other thing I could think of doing.

Night 3

The music was good. The speaker was good. Kris went to the front of the church to pray with the men, and I was proud of him for that. Again, I asked God to give the preacher a message for me. It didn't come, and I sat, crying my eyes out, anxious, with the letter burning in my hands. I began to think maybe this wasn't my time. Maybe it was Kris's time. I was heartbroken. At the end of the service, other people gathered at the stage to sing, and I went to the front of the church with Kris.

I was terrified. I can't explain that kind of fear. The kind where your life isn't in danger, but you feel like you will die anyway. I was shaking and crying and a complete mess. I didn't want these strangers to stare at me, or God forbid, to touch me. But I had this sense of urgency to get rid of my letter, to hand it to someone. (I recognize this now as the Holy Spirit compelling me, using my discomfort to move me forward despite my misgivings.)

I glanced around. Pastor Jason wasn't hard to spot but he was too far away. I saw the assistant pastor, the only one who had really spoken to us during the three nights, a simple hello, but he disappeared into the crowd too. We lingered in the back of the gathering, Kris watching me expectantly, me refusing to go another step until I could control myself. I began to get physically sick. I wanted to throw up. I felt my heart seize up and thought, "Well, I've got to do it before I stroke out in front of everyone." I quickly pushed through to the stage and locked eyes on the one person I didn't want to talk to—the assistant pastor's wife.

She was a tiny bit of a lady, but from the first night, I always knew where she was. She drew attention. She was always dressed to the nines and seemed to always be all over. She stood at the front, in the aisle, talked to anyone and everyone, and what was worse, she had no qualms about worshipping full on, hands up, singing, dancing, and dragging me back to Pentecostal nightmares. My first thought that first night was, "Jeez, lady, calm down."

But this woman *saw* me. There must have been 200 people around me. But she saw *me*. She crossed the stage, reached down, and took the letter I held out. She crouched there waiting for an explanation and all I could muster was, "I need someone to read it." She looked at me, expecting more, but no words came. I was in full-on-panic.

And then, the worst thing happened. She began calling people over. I was surrounded. The guest speaker came over to talk to me. By this time, I was hyperventilating and becoming what I feared most. This preacher was going to put a hand on me, and I was going to fall out in the floor with all these people shouting and speaking in tongues around me. I was just like the lady on that late night televangelist program where crazy things took place and miracles happened.

The preacher started praying for me and asked me to finish the prayer. I can't remember what I said or if it was even discernible. A group of ladies surrounded me and laid their hands on me. I kept expecting to fall out, but I didn't, even though each minute I was sure was the worst torture of my life, until I got to the next minute.

The preacher sat on a bench next to my prayer circle and read my letter. The ladies kept up their praying and added anointing oil. I looked around desperately for Kris. He was somewhere beside me, but out of reach. I then realized what felt like the entire congregation was gathered around staring me down. "Oh no! This is it! This is where the first person to ever die of embarrassment meets her Maker." My legs went weak and numb, and I screamed in my head, "Dear God, please, no!"

The fall out was coming, I was going to faint. I grabbed a lady in front of me, fighting for what I thought was my dignity to the bitter end. She was speaking in my ear, things I didn't understand (I believe she was speaking in tongues), but I was holding on for dear life. I breathed deeply and felt she was safe. I finally looked up at the rafters, the air ducts, anything to focus on other than the masses around me. I gulped air, and I let go. Someone helped me sit on the bench; no one let me fall out. Kris said I stopped shaking. In a blink, it stopped. The terrible tension and panic and tremors that were such a slow and excruciating build just stopped.

I was able to face the preacher and form words. I didn't need to say much. He had read my life story.

He told me to "investigate" God. Knowing from my letter my past occupation, he told me to put all my energy and knowledge and ambition into investigating God. "Investigate that Bible!" He told me to submit. I said, "How can I? God took my daddy—in the worst possible way." The preacher just looked at me flabbergasted. He quoted John 10:10.

"The thief comes to destroy."

He said, "God didn't do that." He talked to Kris about leading and protecting me. He talked about spiritual warfare. He told me that we must be worth something great if we were the focus of so much of the "thief's" energy.

Behind us, on stage, people were being baptized. The preacher asked if I wanted to be baptized. I said, "Is it okay? I've been baptized twice already, and a preacher once told me it looked bad, like I wasn't fully committed the first time." He replied, "Well, he was an ass."

I knew right then I was meant to do it. And if I had to do it 20 times more, I would, because in that moment, I felt different. It was so small, but I felt it so big! I had hope. And so, I was baptized. As the preacher walked me over, he re-introduced me to Pastor Jason and said, "This is your Preacher now." And Kris was also baptized. After, feeling a little silly and slightly embarrassed, I told the preacher that I didn't mean to get everyone riled up. "I'm usually a good Southern Baptist."

Last Night of Revival

The message hit several points for me tonight. Kris dragged me to the front of the church to pray again. I still got anxious, and it was hard to be so vulnerable, on my knees and crying in front of so many people. I kept thinking, they all saw me yesterday and I'm embarrassed at what they must be thinking.

I'm surprised and proud of Kris. I hate to admit that I have never really looked at him in regards to being a spiritual leader of our house. Leader in our field, yes, leader in tactical knowledge, most definitely; but now I see that, for all my upbringing in the Church, he is now more spiritually mature. I feel like I am having to learn all over again.

Hope Restored

And so, Reader, we were relieved. Not completely, but we reached a moment where we could breathe and could finally discern that ever so faint light that had never stopped shining. It grew brighter, still small, but enough warmth to evoke some hope. I slept that night, really slept. My body slipped into a deep sleep to catch up, and we headed to our first normal church service in a few years.

That Sunday after Revival felt like spring. Despite all the setbacks and kicks to the face, it's funny how our spirit can easily slip into hope if we let it. The assistant pastor welcomed us in the entry and told me I looked different. I felt my cheeks go hot in embarrassment, still worried about causing a scene and losing my composure. But it felt good to have reassurance that I wasn't imagining this new chapter.

Others could see it and I was stepping through a door.
A door that could be closed.
A door that could hold back all the
evils, hurts, and misgivings.

I was still a little miffed at God for making it so difficult. "All I wanted was a little sign," I silently hurled up at the ceiling, feeling guilty but willing to prod Him still, even after the relief He granted. As we found our seats, a completely jovial guy bounced up to us and introduced himself as Ryan, another lay pastor. Have I told you how I always felt about "perky" Christians? This time, as annoyed as I might have been, his smile was infectious. He told me he had a message.

As I write this, dear Reader, I have tears streaming down my cheeks. They are a salty mix of shame and joy. For all my doubt, my anger, and my hate, God returned it all in love, and patience, and hope. Ryan told us he had gotten the message the night we were baptized, but said he waited because we were so busy. The message was John 10:10.

> *"The thief comes only to steal and kill*
> *and destroy; I have come that they may*
> *have life, and have it to the full."*

"Don't let anything steal your joy," he said. The visiting preacher had also quoted this to me in prayer the night we were baptized. I was floored. God had answered me.

Returning to my journal, I found notes on one of the speaker's sermons. It was about the lesson on the lake in Matthew 14:22-33. The speaker pointed out that Jesus asked Peter to come to Him on the stormy lake. He asked Peter to step out of the boat in faith. In return, Peter, too, walked on water.

It dawned on me that I had to step out into the aisle and walk my letter to the front of the church in a storm of emotions and strangers. God wanted me to trust in Him and give it all to Him. In return, He spoke to me.

I found hope in another note I wrote.

Sunday after Revival

It was not about the storm. It was about the exorcism on the other side of the lake. I tend to question situations like the storm on the lake. If Jesus, all knowing, knew there would be a storm, why take his disciples through it? Why not wait until it was clear? But Jesus knew that someone on the other side needed help. The storm had to be weathered to reach the other side in time and in preparation. The storms Kris and I weathered were part of our story but were not the main point. In some ways, they may have even been necessary for whatever it is that comes next. I look back on this when I am discouraged, knowing that good things come after the storm.

Leaving church that day, we were revived. A heartbeat could be felt, and we shared a quiet happiness. The decision was made to join the church and make a commitment to refocus on God and try to stop navigating our troubles alone. It wouldn't be easy, as this felt like being born again.

For all our knowledge, we were just babies starting on a journey we thought we had been traveling our whole lives. However, with Revival, we found ourselves being set to right after having traveled down the wrong road.

We opened the new door and stepped through it, new travelers, worn and rugged from misadventures, but fresh faced with hope.

WARFARE

*"It is an unfortunate act that we secure
peace by preparing for war."*
-John F Kennedy

*"For our struggle is not against flesh and blood,
but against the rulers, against the authorities,
against the powers of this dark world and against
the spiritual forces of evil in the heavenly realms."*
-Ephesians 6:12

As I have said before, Reader, there are no coincidences.

After a few tumultuous weeks culminating in a day where I battled my emotions and what seemingly had no other reasonable explanation than a flat-out attack, Kris and I decided to take action. The decision to treat this as a battle was further solidified by the fact that Kris ran out the door to church the following Sunday with his devotional, which was titled, "Sword and Shield." The message at church was titled, "War." Coincidence?

After we were baptized, Kris and I tried to spend more time as family and less time separating into our own little world of hobbies at night. I love to read in bed and like to get there early, although I read late into the night. Kris enjoys playing online video games with a few like-minded ex-military and police friends. The time apart had taken its toll and we put those aside for a while after Revival. But old habits die hard, and when Kris started playing online video games again, with the promise to keep it short and only a couple of times a week, I secretly was glad for the time to read and escape the busy day and duties for a while.

But those couple of times a week doubled. And the nights got later and later. Soon it was back to waking at 2:00 a.m. and realizing Kris wasn't in bed. I would stand in the doorway of the living room glaring at him until he got the message. And then, over time, a small glass of whiskey began to appear next to him. I watched as my husband re-entered "cop-mode" and struggled to snap out of it.

"Cop-mode" or "work-mode" was the self each of us were while on duty. Fully armored and compartmentalized, and a little bit salty, cynical. It was self-preservation mode. A way for us to not connect on too human a level and maintain composure while being screamed at, fought, and viewing the terrible things we had to see. For most of our careers, we each had our commutes and, during that time, we could decompress and snap back into our normal personalities.

Yet, here we were, no longer in law enforcement, yet I was watching my husband fight within himself between the Kris I fell in love with and a bitter Kris who no longer could differentiate between home and a job he no longer had. After a week of inner turmoil, I decided to speak up about my concerns. And when I say speak up, I mean confront. I'm a direct person and was used to dealing with cops and "cop-mode" and could give every bit as much as I got. This approach, I soon found out, was ill-advised.

An Xbox-controller-through-the-tv and screaming match later, I found myself sitting on the floor of our living room, stunned. Kris is the most gentle and loving person I have ever been with. How did we end up here?

During the fight, I looked him dead in his eyes and dead was all I saw. His eyes that are always so green were a dark gray muddy color. There was no light there. A thought came to me that I should just go ahead and deck him, but another voice told me that show of physicality would only escalate things. I was not his wife in this moment. I was someone not falling in line. I would be resisting.

So, I sank to the floor and waited it out, as much as it hurt my pride not to whoop his butt right there for speaking to me the way he did. (Trust me, Reader, he has several inches on me, but I'm a corn-fed country girl and have a few pounds on him and am stronger than I look.) He finally sat on the couch. I climbed in his lap. He talked about having no joy in his life. He talked about ending it. Who was this person? This man who, six months earlier, re-dedicated himself to the Lord?

I pleaded with him to get help. To talk to someone—anyone. He obviously was not over having his livelihood stripped and being found guilty of a crime he did not commit. He wasn't over having his name destroyed and having his friends turn on him to save their own jobs. But mostly, I think he was not over the system he put so much faith in, failing him. As much as he wanted to trust in God and move on, that Xbox game opened a door and let in the old feelings he had put away.

Soon after, we took a trip to our land in West, Texas. It snowed about six inches, and we sat in the trailer as a family, with no distractions, no technology, and for two days, no electricity. We reset and Kris promised to get help. He ended up speaking with Pastor Jason and a new friend, Justin. Both understood having to change careers and putting away police work. It's more than a job to most, it's a life. They sympathized with Kris and validated his feelings.

This whole Xbox incident confirmed something I had been trying to deny for a long time. We were at war. It's more than bad luck, it's more than coincidence. Since joining the church and re-dedicating ourselves, things had gotten increasingly dire in our house. I couldn't ignore it anymore. I used to be of the mindset that God and the Devil had much better things to do than to involve themselves in the inner workings of the Neville's lives. Who are we compared to the world? But the last few months had been utter hell and, although we clung to the church and to our faith, we were losing steam. This incident even brought back instances from my past that seemed—otherworldly.

Please don't judge me, Reader. I am as truthful and honest and rational as you would expect a scientist to be. Some will dismiss what you're about to read as a collection of stories created by an overactive imagination, or my PTSD, or just plain psychosis. But I've sifted through these explanations a hundred times and cannot wholly believe in these diagnoses.

Because there are no coincidences.
Spiritual warfare is real.

LOOKING INTO
THE DARKNESS

———→—————∽———←———

S hortly after witnessing the dead soldier in the tub, as I was
questioning my faith, this happened.

I was standing in my shower at home that so closely mirrored
the bathroom of the dead soldier, and I "saw" blood on the walls, all
the walls, streaming down around me. It was just a flicker—then
nothing. It was more of an impression than anything.

Another time, I walked into my living room and my first death scene
victim was sitting on my love seat, in much the same position he was
in his own recliner, but he was holding his head up, looking at me.
Flashback from PTSD? This was my explanation for many, many
years. But how do you have flashbacks of things you've never seen?
No dead man has ever been seated in my living room, nor has any
blood been spilled in my shower.

In the weeks that followed, as my doubt grew, I began feeling unsafe at night. No reason really, just plain suspicious. One night I heard my patio door open and the blinds rattle. I walked into my living room, gun drawn, and the blinds were indeed moving. I nearly shot out the glass door when I saw my reflection. (Again, Reader, I'm not crazy.) Another time, I was sitting in the living room, and I "saw" a black figure run from my kitchen down the hallway. I could find no people, living or otherwise, when I went to investigate.

The last straw was when I was home alone, again feeling watched, and my fire alarm went off. For a moment I froze, irrationally petrified before coming to my senses and getting up to check the alarm. The moment I stood up from the couch, the alarm went off. I stood in disbelief and looked around. My dog, Mojo, was whining at my feet. I slowly sat down on the couch. No sooner than my butt hit the cushion did the alarm start screaming again. I sat on my couch listening for two minutes before getting the courage to move again. This time when I stood up, the alarm did not stop until I reached for the unit. It never went off again.

By this time, I was sure I needed medication. Any other events that may have happened are lost in the fog of work, medications, therapy, and stress. But they are not the only pre-church events that come to mind when I think of instances designed to shake my faith, my sanity, or both.

Shortly after my daddy died, Gemma, only three years old at the time, was taking a bath. She stood up in the tub and yelled, "Big Poppa!" I was with her, cleaning the bathroom. I immediately felt a sense of dread. It wasn't some warm fuzzy feeling because she recalled his name, or the hope that he was okay. It was dread and terror and a feeling that something was watching me. I asked, "Where, baby?" "Behind you!" she replied. My heart leapt in my chest. Even though every feeling I had said this wasn't my daddy, I said, "You're scaring me, Daddy, you can't be here. I'm sorry."

The Discerning of Spirits

Call me crazy, but I'm being blunt and truthful. I am simply telling you that science cannot explain all things and that, somehow, the Bible has filled in those gaps for me.

> *"Dear friends, do not believe every spirit, but test*
> *the spirits to see whether they are from God, because*
> *many false prophets have gone out into the world."*
> -JOHN 4:1

I have always read this scripture at face value, thinking there are many people who think they have it right, but are in fact misinterpreting God's Word and spreading their false information. But perhaps Jesus meant something unseen.

Those little voices that speak lies into our minds. The doubts that creep in and spread like wildfire. Tiny demons with pitchforks, poking and prodding and driving us off the straight and narrow. I believe there are forces, whether you call them spirits, ghosts, entities, whatever, that cannot be explained, and that, every so often, we see in a glimpse or a flicker. They are a challenge. They are not of God, and because of that, they are darkness.

Sometimes these "sightings" become a strange comfort for us. A sign that things go on. In fact, despite feeling fear when Gemma "saw" Daddy in the bathroom, I convinced myself it was a sign that he was there and letting me know he was okay. I had even written as much in this very book, but after some counsel and deep reflection, I realized I needed to test the spirits. So, in my experience, these spirits, these flickers that have only caused fear and confusion, cannot be for good. I don't rule out the possibility of good spirits, angels, if you will, but I stay wary.

I can't recall when it started, but both Gemma and Gage have had terrible nightmares in our house. Not just bad dreams where they wake up crying, but night terrors. Gemma seems to be the most affected. Even times when she is in bed with us, she will sit up, eyes wide, screaming incoherently. She claws the air and fights against us, staring past and not really seeing us.

One weekend, I attended a church event where I brought up the topic that our family might be under spiritual attack. After returning home, I was talking to Kris about whether we were crazy, or if we should get the house "cleansed" or blessed. Gemma was asleep on the couch, and as we talked, she started whimpering. Before I could reach her, she was in full blown panic, staring past me again, still asleep, but eyes wide open. She kicked and hit at me. Finally, my five-year-old girl who only had five months of Sunday school lessons yelled, "Jesus!" And just like a snap, she curled back up and went back to sleep.

It was this event that sealed the deal for us.

Kris walked the house one night, reading scripture. Shortly after, he left on an overnight trip to help my mom. I got an awful feeling and was downright scared. Remember, Reader, I've seen it all and I don't scare easily. I gathered the kids in my bed and walked the house and prayed out loud. I played scripture through my phone as we slept. No bad dreams.

Another night Gage woke up screaming. We heard a loud thud as he jumped from his bed to the floor and ran to the nursery door, banging on it until we rushed out of our room, ready to rescue him and vanquish anything nefarious in the process. Once he calmed down, he told us he dreamed there was a bee with sharp teeth eating his hands. I said, "Bubba, bees don't have teeth! Where have you ever seen a bee with teeth?" I was trying to be reassuring in my silliness. What he said next made my blood run cold. "A bad angel came and read me a story about it."

We hadn't broached the subject of hell or demons with either Gemma or Gage. The only mention of angels had been about Big Poppa and about how God sends His angels to protect them. I grabbed a Bible and asked God to show me something, anything, that would help explain what happened. My first thought was to turn to the ribbon marker. My second thought was, "That's too easy." So, ignoring that small thought, as I often do, I turned to a random page and didn't find anything to help. Surprise, surprise. I turned to the ribbon, and it bookmarked John 10.

> *"The man who does not enter through the gate but*
> *climbs in some other way is a thief and robber."*

We reassured Gage that God would never send a bad angel. And we didn't say anything about the devil. We simply told him that he had a bad dream.

Generational Curses

After speaking with a few people at church, we believed our house harbored some awful things. I'm not talking Amityville Horror haunted. Just darkness clinging to the walls and corners. Dark places where things like sadness, grief, anger, and hate can grow.

My paternal grandfather, "Papa," was an alcoholic. Not just an alcoholic. A raging one. And not raging like he drank a fifth of whiskey for breakfast (although I'm sure that happened). But raging, as in anger. Blinding, red hot, blackout anger. I always thought he must have been raised in an abusive house. He had been terrible to both my daddy and my grandmother when Daddy was little. My daddy had scars he wouldn't talk about. But there were stories about hiding from Papa … a story about Daddy and my grandmother crouched in the culvert at the end of the driveway listening to Papa screaming in rage and hearing gunshots. I could also see the scars and emotions from stories he didn't tell. I asked him once if Papa had been beaten as a child and he said, "No, there was just something wrong in his head."

When I was almost three years old, we lived down the street from my Papa's house. He had gotten into an argument with my daddy one day and gotten really drunk. He called Daddy and told him something to the effect that he was going to come over and kill us all. I have one clear memory of that day. Through the screen door, I saw my Papa climb the steps of our house. I was then scooped up and pressed against a wall. I could see the hallway and pictures, but I couldn't move. And that's all I remember.

I'm told that, on that day, my Papa came into our house with a gun. My daddy scooped me up—he protected me—and he shot his own father in self-defense. This is why my daddy means so much to me. This is also why I feel like our house harbors something dark. I don't feel like the house is evil—it's just a house. But whatever demons my Papa struggled with, well, maybe they didn't all clear out after his death. After all, the Bible does talk about generational curses.

"Yet he does not leave the guilty unpunished; he punishes the children and their children for the sin of the parents to the third and fourth generation."
-EXODUS 34:7

"This day I call the heavens and the earth as witnesses against you that I have set before you life and death, blessings and curses. Now choose life, so that you and your children may live."
-DEUTERONOMY 30:19

I do not know enough to go into depth here, but I don't think God punishes us for things our ancestors have done. However, I do believe our choices have consequences, and sometimes those consequences are far reaching. You may scoff. But think about it scientifically. We know abuse victims oftentimes become abusers themselves. Things like addiction, alcoholism, even struggles with relationships are passed on. These things are not wholly genetic. They can be learned behaviors that affect several generations, in some cases.

And what more are these things, but curses? A curse to live a life where anger and physical aggression are the only ways someone knows to express themselves? A curse to be tied to a substance or drink so one can feel like living? A curse to stay in an unhealthy situation because that is all one knows?

Again, I don't have it all figured out, Reader, but I do know my Papa's actions affected my daddy, they affected me, and I am willing to do anything I can to ensure that the "cycle" (just a scientific way of saying "curse") is broken. It is one thing to read this chapter incredulously. It is an entirely different thing to pick your sleeping daughter up from the couch to take her to bed and have her awaken, screaming, with eyes wide open, staring and pointing into a dark corner, unable to explain what she is seeing or doing.

So, when all science and logic escaped us, Kris opened the door, I told Gemma to say, "Get out," and then we prayed in Jesus' name.

And where all science and logic failed,
Jesus let the entire house get a good night's sleep.

THE DARKNESS
LOOKS BACK

———◦———

These "sightings" were not the only "mysterious" things that happened. Our health and finances have also been affected in ways that go beyond explanation.

The weekend after Revival, I was not feeling well, starting with Sunday service. Mama needed us to mow, so I pushed down the throbbing pain in my left side, and hopped on the tractor, hoping to knock out the 15 acres of pasture while Kris used the weed-eater on the five acres around the yard, barn and shop. I put on Christian music for the first time in my life.

After three hours, I hopped off the tractor and promptly threw up. Later that night, I woke up in agony. Because of Covid restrictions, I knew Kris could not take me to the emergency room, so I drove myself the 45 minutes to the hospital, praying I would not pass out. Diagnosis: kidney stone. No explanation why, just a random, tiny stone making its way out.

At the time, I didn't think anything sinister about it, just my horrible luck. The next day Kris wanted to go to the men's group at church and told me I should go to the women's group. I'm kind of a lone wolf, Reader, so I wasn't as excited as he was at the prospect of talking to people. I took some medicine for the kidney issues and tagged along. About 15 minutes into the meeting, I knew I was in trouble.

That kidney stone was wreaking havoc. I stayed another five minutes, choking back tears, until the pain was too much to bear. I motioned to someone and asked her to get my husband for me. By the time we got home, I was screaming. This time, I knew there would be no driving myself. We called an ambulance so the kids wouldn't have to sit in the car for hours. A good move since this time I was admitted.

I spent the week in a hospital bed with a stent. Surgery was scheduled for that weekend. I tried to remain optimistic. I tried to stay in the Word. I even pulled up an online service from our church. The minute the pastor started speaking, I violently threw up. And so it went. Important Sundays or just when I'd start to feel at home with worship, *bam*! Another kidney stone.

After several flair ups and against my own hesitations, I had a lady at church pray over me. It was suggested that she had a "healing anointing." I felt silly at the time, letting this woman I barely knew lay hands on me, my scientific mind scoffing at my desperate attempt to stop the pain. But I went kidney stone free for over a month. Then, lo, another kidney stone cropped up on my way to church several weeks later, and this time I needed surgery. At the time of this writing, I have passed nine kidney stones and have had two kidney-related surgeries.

I hear you say, "Oh, Amy, that's just health issues." Is it Reader?

There are no coincidences.

The Thief Tries Another Tactic

After the Xbox incident, and after speaking with Pastors Jason and Justin, Kris started feeling better about giving up police life. He sold the Xbox. He took off his thin blue line ring. The thin blue line is a symbol amongst law enforcement of holding the line between evil and good. A line that your brothers and sisters in blue all hold together, keeping people safe. Standing in that line between chaos and darkness and order and light. And he unfollowed police pages on social media. He decided against joining the safety team at church. As much as it hurt him, he was being obedient.

Then we got an automated call from the probation office saying we were delinquent on our payment, and we had three days to remit a payment of over $500. Remember, for the "assault and oppression charge," Kris was given 12 months' probation with fees and other add-ons. Mind you, Kris had called six months earlier to see when the first payment was due. He was told that, due to Covid, they were behind. Then they said, "We'll call you."

When I tell you I had a meltdown, that's probably an understatement. Sorry, but I have to yell this part, Reader:

WE HAVE BEEN LAW ABIDING CITIZENS
AND CIVIL SERVANTS FOR OUR ENTIRE
ADULT LIVES AND MY HUSBAND WAS
WRONGLY PROSECUTED, PERSECUTED,
AND CONVICTED. BUT HE SWALLOWED
IT AND HAS DONE EVERYTHING ASKED.
WHAT MORE DO YOU PEOPLE WANT?!!!

Kris was on a job with little cell service and called to ask for my help tracking down the right person to talk to in the probation office. He was calm, but I could hear the fear in his voice. He said, "I can't violate, Amy. I can't go to jail." So, I started making calls. No one in the county offices where the "offense" took place could or would answer my questions. I called the county we live in, and they said they had received transfer paperwork, but Kris was not officially a "client" yet. I called the initial county offices back. I was told for the first time that Kris had a probation officer assigned to him. One he was never told about. We found out that his probation had in fact started five months earlier, so we weren't just a little late. We were months late.

I still could not get a call back from his new probation officer, so I contacted her supervisor who told me the officer was out of the office until the following week. I asked how it could happen that he was on probation and had received no calls. She did not have an answer. None of this made sense. There was no explanation other than outside forces. No one at adult probation drops the ball for over five months.

Even though I still tend to view situations through a scientific lens, I think there are key times when we are susceptible to spiritual warfare.

**The Devil may not be behind every misfortune,
but, in my lifetime, I can see where he laid his hooves down.
At my weakest points when faith was
a flicker, I got kicked hard.
A little final push toward the cliff's edge.
Or when my faith was its strongest
and the prospect of losing another
wretched soul was in danger,
he would strike out with an especial furor.**

Why not the times in between?

Well, Reader, complacency is one of his best tools.

When you think you are doing alright, following an easy road and wide path, you only realize you're going in the wrong direction when it's too late. Not all his wiles are spent on outright attacks and schemes. The simplest plans are often the best. And we humans do a pretty good job of separating ourselves from God and that narrow path.

In our complacency we forget he exists. What's the old saying? His best trick, right?

THE ENEMY

———⟶———⟿———⟵———

At the time of writing, we passed the three-year anniversary of my daddy's death. It was on a Sunday morning, March 4, when I threw on my uniform and stood in the mud trying to figure out his accident, as if solving it would bring him back, make him whole.

For about a week leading up to the anniversary, I had terrible nightmares. I call them flashbacks, but again, how can you have a flashback of something you've never seen? Daddy was gone by the time I arrived. But in my flashback I see him in the mud, steam coming off his leathers (protective gear to prevent road rash in the event of an accident), his breath foggy in the night air as he coughs up blood.

And even though I know, I know, beyond any shadow of a doubt that my daddy was dead before he left the road, I see him suffer. I feel guilt that I wasn't the one to find him. I'm angry that I didn't get to say goodbye, that I didn't get to hold his hand and be with him in those final moments. I'm upset at the fear and pain he must have felt (that I logically, scientifically know didn't happen). Does any of this make sense, Reader? This huge contradiction of facts, feelings, and misgivings? This jumble that fear makes possible?

On the anniversary of the last time I was with my daddy, I was voluntold to go to the Motorcycle Ministry at church. The Motorcycle Ministry! I went, cried a lot, made a mess of myself, but was able to fellowship with the most awesome, understanding people you could ever meet.

And then anniversary Sunday came. To honor Daddy, I decided to wear one of his shirts to church. I did look for excuses not to go, to lay in bed. But I put on the shirt, and I went. During praise and worship (live music during the first 30 minutes of church), I had to push those awful thoughts out of my head—my daddy, my stress, my own disappointment, my doubts—just a constant bombardment of distraction. I prayed to God to banish anything not of Him. Anything evil or unclean. I needed and wanted to focus. And nothing happened. My heart was still broken, my head still refused to pay attention, and my anger was still building.

A thought came to me. Just a quiet little bit of a thing, but bright. Not loud, but bright. Like a spotlight in the dark, my flashlight on a crime scene, uncovering evidence.[3] "You are in church. There is nothing here to be afraid of. You are safe." Then what in the Hell, Heaven, or Earth is it? I realized the only thing standing in my head, in that moment, was me. I am my own worst enemy.

> Imagine there are two monsters standing in front you
> to defeat and both could be defeated with sword and

shield. One of the monsters has a terrible face but the other has a face you recognize and love. Which would be harder to defeat? Which fight scares you more? It is one thing to go to war against an enemy that looks the part. It is another to face one that looks like you.

It is easy to see the devil behind every corner, every bad day or accident. It is easy to place blame on someone or some other. But why should anyone fear the devil, knowing the power of Jesus and having faith in God? The devil only has the power any one person allows him to have. He is invited in or finds an open door, or even a crack. He uses our own fears against us. I know that with faith and a word nothing evil can stand.

"Resist the devil and he
will flee from you."
-JAMES 4:7

But myself? She is a much more devious enemy.

I know all my flaws, fears, and misgivings. I know all my questions and doubts. And most of all, I know all the excuses I believe. I can pick myself apart faster than my four-year-old can destroy my freshly folded laundry. I can conjure up images to make a grown man terrified of the dark. I can beat myself black and blue with nothing but regret. I can make every scientific argument ever taught in modern universities. I can, "but why?" for forever and a day. I can excuse myself out of prayer, church, faith, friendship, and love.

I can say the devil made me do it but who let him in? I can sit all day and talk about every bad thing that has happened to me, Reader, and I can tell you it was the devil. But that is a dangerous thing. We must be able to discern those things we can control and those things we can't. Those things within our control: our thoughts, our hobbies, our faith, our obedience, must be attended to. If we do not attend to these with the same, if not more, vigilance than this fear of the devil, we are sabotaging ourselves. To ignore these or to pass them off as the devil's work is keeping a wound open and festering.

It has been the same with my heart. I can tell you the devil sends me horrible dreams. But the truth is, Reader, I made them. I let every accident I ever worked become my daddy's accident. I let every injury in his autopsy report become visual. I let my fear, my hurt, and my anger fester. I blamed everyone and everything for this sadness and this pain. And as I write, I am sobbing with the hurt. I wish I could blame the devil. If I blamed the devil, I could keep this pain. I could hang on to this sorrow.

"Okay, well, we knew this was going to happen. She has officially lost it. *Keep her sorrow?*" Is that what you're thinking, Reader? Am I crazy? Look at it this way: Why do we grieve longer than we should? Why do we hold on to bad habits? Why do we harbor addiction? Why do we fall off the wagon? Why don't we say we're sorry? Why don't we forgive?

We all find some comfort in familiarity. We are creatures of habit. And habits form addictions and cravings and eventually familiarity. And once you feel at home in something, it's hard to escape the evil you know...

Sitting in church, everyone singing around me, I changed my prayer. I prayed for God to help me keep my attention on Him. I looked up at the cross and begged God to help me stop myself. And instantly, after three years, my heart was warm. I could feel it being stitched up. After every sermon, every prayer, every tear, and every rock turned over, I found my answer.

The feeling wasn't fleeting. The anniversary of his death, a day I had come to dread, came as it always does. The last two years I was a sobbing mess and had barely gotten through the days. This third year, I exchanged hugs with a few close coworkers as they gave me encouraging words. I asked God to get me through the day and asked Him to tell Daddy how much he was missed and loved. I played music for my students and we had a relaxing project day.

And then, I was blessed twice! I scheduled an important phone call regarding the publication of this book, and I came across a much desired and needed job opportunity! Later that day I ran into the assistant pastor's wife in the church parking lot. I asked her to pray for me and for this new opportunity. Even though I hesitated, she grabbed my hands without a second thought, and we prayed as people were coming out the door. She said the fact all these things happened on the anniversary of Daddy's death wasn't insignificant.

Sometimes, we must face dark things and battle against the Devil, and sometimes we must stop our own selves from demolishing all the good things God wants for us.

A preacher can bless my house in Jesus' name and banish every dark thing. An anointed sister can lay her hands in Jesus' name and pray away a kidney stone. But only I can recognize myself. And only Jesus can help me defeat my own worst enemy.

PART III

REVELATION

"Here I am!
I stand at the door and knock.
If anyone hears my voice and opens the door,
I will come in and eat with that person,
and they with me."

REVELATION 3:20

THE WORST BOOK
OF THE BIBLE

—————— ✦ ✦ ⤳ ✦ ——————

"I cry out to you, God, but you do not answer;
I stand up, but you merely look at me."
-JOB 30:20

It's funny how the Lord will make you so uncomfortable you have no choice but to act. So, while I was busy waiting for Him to speak to me directly, He was throwing sign after sign my way, and eventually slapped me upside the head … with the book of Job.

Let me tell you about the book of Job. It is literally the worst. Lord, forgive me! (Is that blasphemy?) Job was a man who had it all: wife, kids, family, and many earthly blessings. Well, the Devil decided to test Job's love for God and literally rained hellfire down upon him. Job lost everything, including his health. For every misfortune he faced, his faithfulness was rewarded in the end, and then some.

But still, I really disliked that book.

Job was not a bad guy who deserved a little misfortune. By all accounts, he was a decent and well-liked man. I always had a hard time understanding how God could let this happen to one of His children. My daddy had a hard time understanding it, too. So, in the past, I generally avoided Job, lest I be forced to think too hard about it.

A week or so after Revival, while talking to Brother Joey about the kidney stones and getting sick whenever I tried to watch a sermon, he said Kris and I should study from Job. I told him it was the absolute worst. Big mistake. I suppose it's blasphemous to say such things. But Reader, I am being honest with you. Thankfully, the Lord didn't take my blaspheme too seriously. But He did decide to use it as a lesson.

A Meltdown

In the summer of 2020, with the political climate stacked high against police officers, we received word that the appeals court had reached a final decision on Kris's case. They upheld the conviction. The reasoning was so baseless and backwards to anything the justice system stood for that, if it wasn't so heartbreaking, it would have been funny. The document we read stated, "It was not the burden of the prosecution to prove excessive force." Really? So it's "guilty until proven innocent?" Our entire justice system was founded on one principle that these judges ignored.

In that moment, I lost all steam. The physical pain and kidney stones I could deal with. The injustice—I couldn't. My chest filled with that familiar PTSD tightness and my heart took up residence in my throat. Every hope I had for the future disappeared in a flash.

We would never regain Kris's retirement and financial earnings. We would never regain his good name. We would never get the chance to set the record straight. Kris would be branded in the public's eye and there was nothing we could do. Out of money, out of resources, this was the end of the line. Our last-ditch effort had failed. Not only that but we also worried what this precedent would do for other officers. Officers who found themselves in similar situations.

I immediately prayed and asked God to help me. The panic building inside told me I was going to have a meltdown. I reached out to the assistant pastor and his wife (the very same woman I tried to avoid at Revival), and they called us. Kris, who apparently missed the memo about how awful this was, was calm and accepting. As he spoke to them over the phone, he was peaceful, and he did not express my panic to them. I told them how I felt, as I continuously blew my nose and sobbed. We promised to make it to church the next night, and they promised to have the elders pray over us and to help us more in person. At this point, I was still not completely open to having a mob prayer session, so I didn't know whether I felt better or worse after speaking with them.

I cried myself to sleep that night while Kris stayed up and prayed. He asked God to show him what he needed to learn and read. He opened the Bible to a random page. What page, you ask? *The first page of the book of Job.* The next morning, I posted something on Facebook to the effect of "woe is me." Brother Duane mentioned the book of Job on my post and Kris posted about his revelation. And while they praised God, I sat amongst my snotty tissue paper mountain and sulked, because the book of Job is the absolute worst.

At the advice of my friend Sandi, I reached out to Pastor Jason, who, along with his wife, were ex-law enforcement. I was given Pastor Jason's wife's number and I called her. I spilled my guts and she had some encouraging words. We agreed to see each other at church that night.

Despite having several people encourage me, I had a hard time keeping it together. By the afternoon I was downright bitter. I decided to pay Sandi a visit to wallow some more. I could not understand how this mess could be God's plan. Wasn't Kris in a much better position to help people and do God's work when he was a police officer? Weren't we having a bigger impact in law enforcement? And now, he was convicted of assault and my head was so full of ghosts, neither of us could do what we spent over a decade building up.

At some point, Job weaseled his way into the conversation. I went on a rant about how terrible the book of Job is. I asked Sandi, "If God is supposed to be so active in our lives, and if He loves us so much, how could He let any of that happen to Job? To us?" Her reply stung and I knew it was the truth.

"God is not a puppet master."

The Lord did not create us to be pawns in a cosmic game. And while He has plans and gives us gifts and a guide (the Bible) to use along our journey, He allows us to make our own way. It is a gift to be able to write our own story. The catch is, we are great at taking the wrong roads. He does not wish to control every aspect of our lives.

He wishes for us to use our free will and He guides us. How simple it would be if He directed our every move—and how absolutely boring.

The greatest things in life come with experience and the greatest joy comes from knowing great pain. Life would be meaningless if God pulled our strings and made our decisions for us. Life is a beautiful lesson that can only be learned by living. And living can only truly occur when we are free to decide.

Also, faithfulness cannot be born in predestined fate. God wants us to choose Him. The only way for that to happen is to give us free will. Like any parent, it hurts to see our children make choices we know aren't good for them. However, sometimes we must let our children make their own mistakes. In this, they learn, they grow, and hopefully, they choose better in the future.

> *"You, my brothers and sisters, were called to be free.*
> *But do not use your freedom to indulge the flesh;*
> *rather, serve one another humbly in love."*
> -GALATIANS 5:13

We have been given freedom; we must choose love over sin.

The sermon that night was on self-control. By all appearances I should have been safe from having to think about how horrible the book of Job is. But the Lord works in mysterious ways and the lay pastor ended the service with a book of Job reference.

Sandi, about seven rows in front of us, turned and snickered at me.

THE BEST BOOK
IN THE BIBLE

—◦❧◦—

F inally taking a hint, I determined to figure out the book
of Job.

> *"In the land of Uz there lived a man whose*
> *name was Job. This man was blameless and*
> *upright; he feared God and shunned evil."*
> -JOB 1:1

Job had a period of trial wherein the Devil tested him, to prove a
point to God that only those who have been blessed love the Lord.

> *"Have you not put a hedge around him and his*
> *household and everything he has? You have blessed*
> *the work of his hands, so that his flocks and*
> *herds are spread throughout the land. But now*

*stretch out your hand and strike everything he
has, and he will surely curse you to your face."*
-JOB 1:10-11

The Devil argued that if Job was to face hardship, his faith would fail.

The first tribulations Job faced were the killings of his servants, his sheep were burned by lightning, his camels were stolen by raiders, and his children were killed while eating supper as their home collapsed on them. I know what you are thinking—first tribulations?

Trust me, Reader, I was right there with you. But Job, ever faithful, fell to his knees and prayed and worshipped. And so, the Devil needed a new plan.

*"Skin for skin!" Satan replied. "A man will
give all he has for his own life. But now stretch
out your hand and strike his flesh and bones,
and he will surely curse you to your face."*
-JOB 2:4-5

The Devil argued that Job still had his health, but there is no strife like being ill and in pain. Surely Job would no longer sing the Lord's praises if his body failed him.

Have you ever been in serious pain? With my history of surgery and kidney stones, believe me when I say, most times I was screaming, "God!" But my screams were always accompanied by numerous other words of the four-letter variety. Pain tends to wipe the mind and command all the attention. And so, Job was afflicted with boils from head to toe.

It was at this point where Job's wife threw in the towel. She scolded Job for his faith while it seemed to her God had forsaken him. Dear Job scolded her right back and kept praying. Now alone and ill, Job began to question his existence. Do you blame him, Reader? And does it not hit close to home when you consider all the times you've questioned your very own existence for far less troubles? It does to me.

In fact, I think now maybe my avoidance of this book wasn't because of its sadness but because of my own shame. The book of Job runs the gamut of feelings and doubt I had been running from for so long.

> He wondered what he had done wrong.
> He wondered why God would do this to him.
> He doubted God's nature.
> He debated with his friends and tried to reason away
> his troubles.

It is here, in their debating, many questions of doubt are addressed.

> Why do bad things happen?
> Why does good sometimes come to those who are wicked?
> What is God's nature?

And God provides answers as He speaks to Job after so many misfortunes. God challenges Job's reasoning and, after making His point, Job realizes his folly. Job had disregarded all good in the world that came from God, while not one horrible event that occurred was God's doing.

How many times have I disregarded every good and true gift in my hardships? How many times did I think God was behind them?

In my daddy's death, I had forgotten he was a gift, and I had a lifetime of memories from our time together. I spent countless hours trying to understand why God would take him in such a violent way. In such a way that would devastate my soul, reading the autopsy and trying to find a way to minimize his injuries to my mama.

In my pain and struggle with fertility, I had forgotten the new strength I found and medical knowledge I gained. I disregarded the fact that I was gifted with motherhood and that I was able to conceive naturally after the treatments and Gemma's birth. Gage would not be here if I had not had to endure IVF the first time.

In all the haunting memories of cases worked, I failed to see the good that came from speaking with a victim, from advocating for a child, from giving a family peace or justice. Those crimes were not the work of God. They were the work of evil because we can choose, and not everyone chooses good. The Devil wouldn't have a job creating havoc if we didn't have free will or if we all chose God. And his evil deeds are like dropping a pebble in a pond, the ripples continue outward and reach the far banks. We all are bound to come across a ripple, even if we choose God, all our actions can affect others.

As I struggled with knowing there was nothing I could do to comfort my mama when her father, my Papa, died on the floor of our family home, I forgot how his wish to be kept out of a nursing home had been granted. I had forgotten all the extra time he had with Gemma, Gage, and me on those afternoons spent with him.

And as I write this, Reader, I am crying. I am crying for all the times I could have called that Good by its name: God.

How many times could I have borne witness to His faithfulness, even in the middle of a violent, chaotic crime? How many times did I fail to thank Him for my blessings? And could it possibly be that part of my grief, an overwhelming guilty part, is because I did not cherish and be grateful for my family, friends, and livelihood? Wouldn't letting Daddy go be so much easier if I rejoiced in our time together, never taking a single moment for granted, and had faith that it was his time?

As I came to these realizations, Job came to his own. He repented to God and prayed for not only himself, but for others. Because of his repentance, God rewarded Job more than he ever had.

On Sunday after the court decision, I made my way to the front of the church and admitted I could not let go of the court conviction and what it would mean for us. As Brother Duane and Sister Brandey prayed with Kris and me, I sank to my knees, and I recalled how Pastor Jason told me it was time to let Kris fight the battles he chooses. I stubbornly resolved to be soft and to look to my husband. He had decided this battle was not worth fighting. We needed to save our energy for more worthy causes, and I needed to return the pants to Kris.

The book of Job ends with a happily ever after:

> *"So Job died, being old and full of days."*
> -JOB 42:17

I know my story will end in a happily ever after, no matter how it started, no matter what comes between. I'm sure I will stumble along the way; but for the moment, I am peaceful and, dare I say, happy? I am full of hope that should I stumble, should doubt creep in, I have a steadfast husband, a church family, and a patient Father.

And that is how the worst book in the Bible became the best guide in figuring out life.

GOD'S VOICE

———— ✦ ————

I n the beginning of this book, I touched on how sad I felt knowing God would not speak to me. My entire life I wished God would just come out and say what I should be doing. I never could understand why He stopped speaking to His people. The Bible is filled with stories of God speaking with His chosen ones. I was downright jealous.

Then one Sunday, Pastor Jason talked about God changing tactics, like fishermen did lures. If He wasn't getting through to His people using one method, why would it surprise us that He changed the bait? Pastor Jason was speaking about how the Church and the congregation was evolving. He talked about the type of people being called to minister. I started wondering, "Did God just change His tactic?"

In this modern world where technology has brought the world's knowledge to the palm of our hands, oftentimes, the first instinct is to find a "rational explanation." I am growing to abhor this phrase, as if God is not a "rational" explanation. But it is true. Human nature and curiosity lead us to dissect and analyze and explain away things we don't understand.

I am a scientist. I look at the world with a lens of discovery. For years, my job was to turn chaos into an explanatory chain of events to help a jury understand a crime. Science has allowed humans to organize the world into neat little packages that can be studied and understood. It has allowed us to quell our fear of the unknown by explaining away phenomena that for centuries were seen as paranormal, other-worldly, and even miracles.

As with most things, the more we think we know about a particular subject, the more we think we can figure it all out. And those things we cannot figure out? We fear. Strange lights in the sky, the mind of a psychopath, an unsolved mystery—that which we cannot explain or understand tends to frighten us.

Imagine how modern man would react if we saw a bush burst into flames! Did I mention that it was also talking? What would we do if a winged man swooped down and said, "I have a message for you"? How trigger happy would we get? I think God, being the loving and patient Father He is, has taken our growth and discoveries into consideration. I believe He speaks to each of us in different ways and uses methods tailored to our level of comfort with the mystical.

The Bible describes God's voice throughout:

"And behold, the glory of the God of Israel was coming from the east. His voice was like the roar of rushing waters, and the land was radiant with his glory."
-EZEKIEL 43:2

"The LORD thundered from heaven; the voice of the Most High resounded."
-PSALM 18:13

In Exodus, Psalm, and Revelation, God's voice is often described as "thunder."

The way we hear God is as individual as our fingerprints, custom tailored to fit our walk with Him. Some might hear an actual voice; some may see visions or have dreams. But the scientist that I am would probably not be able to tolerate these things without running to the nearest psychologist.

Can you imagine our reactions if a mysterious voice just popped out of nowhere saying, "Are you sure you want to do that?" It reminds me of a song my daddy loved by Ray Wylie Hubbard called, *"Conversation with the Devil."*[4] It is based on an actual dream he had one night where he found himself in hell facing eternity. At the end of the song, Ray Wylie Hubbard wakes up. He penned, "I took this dream as a sign from God, so I thought I better pray, 'Don't ever speak to me directly, thanks anyway.'"

I am learning that God speaks to me in the most subtle of ways. A song, a sign, a feeling, a nagging thought. It is a very unobtrusive way of speaking. I am sure there have been numerous times a sign has swept right by me, but I am learning to be ever watchful. As I've stated before, there are no coincidences, not in crime scene, and not with the Lord. The signs I have paid attention to have been profound and, while I have searched for any other explanation, none fit, other than the Lord is speaking to me. And He speaks in a voice that hasn't sent me running for the hills.

When my daddy was killed, Gemma was only three and Gage two, so we were unsure how to approach the subject of death with them. The first week, we said nothing. We found a babysitter for the funeral and if the kids asked, we just responded, "Poppa's not home." The day after the funeral, we drove by the cemetery with the kids in tow, to arrange the flowers. We still had not told the babies anything. When I got back in the truck, tears in my eyes, Gemma, looking out the window at the flowers, said "Poppa's in the garden." This was one of those tested moments that left me feeling peaceful. I thank God for the brief glimpse that my daddy was okay in the days following his death.

There have been times when my crime scene knowledge has come back to haunt me. After reading the autopsy, I could "see" my daddy. I know exactly what those types of injuries look like. I know how far he was thrown, and I know the mechanics of the wreck. I get upset at the thought of him lying so broken in the field and that I was not with him. I feel guilt at times at being the last one to know about his passing. What scares me the most is wondering if he was conscious. Did he lie there awake? Did he know he was dying? Was he scared? Was he in terrible pain?

I was driving home from work one afternoon, sobbing uncontrollably, overwhelmed by these questions. I could not handle the thought of my daddy in pain. I kept asking God why. I screamed at the windshield, "Was he hurting?" At that moment, a song my daddy and I loved to play and sing together came on the radio. *Comfortably Numb* by Pink Floyd.

Again, I don't believe in coincidences!

Every day I spend leaning on Him, His voice is clearer. Not any louder, but more easily recognizable. I can almost differentiate between Him, myself, and the Liar. I think it takes practice to communicate and, with time and dedication, I will see and hear more. Because maybe, just maybe, God softened His voice. He has adopted a way to speak to our hearts in such a way that promotes patience, love and understanding, but also requires us to be attentive students. He gave us His Word.

> *"In the beginning was the Word, and the Word*
> *was with God, and the Word was God."*
> -JOHN 1:1

And He gave us an internal voice to carry with us.

> *"And I will ask the Father, and he will give you*
> *another advocate to help you and be with you forever."*
> -JOHN 14:16

_____

The next time you are looking for a burning bush,
maybe try being still.
Listen to the whisper,
read the Word.
He will be there.

_____

WALKING
IN FAITH

Yes, God will always be there, but He does want us to meet Him. Like me wanting a sign at Revival and having to trust Him and walk that letter to the front of the church, He wants everyone to take a step. He will cross oceans and mountains and vast distances. He already did on the cross, but He wants to see that tiny step. Like Peter, stepping onto the water, Jesus granted him the impossible, which was only marred by his doubt.

The more we trust, the more we gain.
The further we walk in faith,
the more blessed and peaceful we can be in any circumstance,
even impossible ones!

I hope you don't dismiss anything I've said, believing I have knowledge you don't, or that I have experiences you don't. I am a normal person going through life like the next person. Please don't think, Reader, that this book came together flawlessly and that I had some special insight or ability.

I have written my thoughts and feelings and my own theories, only to be gently corrected and shown I have been guilty of putting words in God's mouth. I have misinterpreted and faltered. I have given up too many times to count. Walking in faith is not easy. The road signs aren't highlighted on yellow or green billboards. It takes stamina, discipline, fellowship, and maintenance. I owe a lot of people a lot of credit for helping me interpret my thoughts, God's signs, and for encouraging me to keep on the road.

After the court conviction against Kris and to help with finances, I began working part-time in the church nursery every Sunday morning, Monday night, and Wednesday night. When I took this on, it was a huge blessing! I felt pride in giving back to the church and was relieved we had some help financially. Before the part-time job, we had gone to church three times a week where I was continually reminded to speak with God and to lean on Him. I was being taught lessons from all manner of different people and walks.

With this new job in church, I was in the nursery with the babies instead of in the worship service with my family. Little did I know how hard it would be to walk in faith when I lacked the stamina to maintain a "long distance relationship" with God. Without being in the church services every other day, I forgot to talk to God. I began to feel disconnected. I still sang during praise and worship time, but the

songs lost their power. I didn't connect with the words, I didn't cry —
for joy or otherwise. The fervor was not there. I gradually slipped
back into a place of gray, where I prayed almost as an afterthought.
I put God on the warmer and I suffered for it. I was not as joyful. I
noticed an uptick in my anxiety and worry. I felt isolated for the first
time since Revival. And my old friend, shame, came to visit. I was
ashamed I had slipped backwards in my walk. I allowed God's voice
to become a mere whisper that was easy to ignore.

And so, I realize walking in faith takes maintenance, dear Reader.
It takes dedicating time to read and study. Every pastor worth his
salt will say this. I spent my whole life making excuses for not
reading the Bible. But the Bible is God's true voice. His instruction
manual for life. I have also come to know that dedicating time
to read and study takes encouragement. I need to be helped with
scriptures and lessons. I need to be in church to get those nuggets of
knowledge and hear interpretations and connections to encourage
me to delve deeper. To investigate further. If I am not fed these
tidbits and morsels, it's easy to forget I am starving.

Fighting Against Doubt

In the midst of this struggle where I was distant, I began to doubt
my own words. Reader, forgive me, but the words about finding
and recognizing God's voice began to lose its shine. In my distance,
I started to struggle with my own belief and conviction about the
things God revealed to me. That needling doubt that began with a
crime scene and consumed my life, the doubt I supposedly closed the
door on, was easy to let back in.

I began this book because I felt called to share our story. Once I started writing, words just spilled out. Not to say I didn't have serious revision and struggles with some topics, but it was easy, and it felt good. But I stopped writing because I wasn't diligent. I ran out of fuel. Writer's block. It could only be one thing: I stopped seeking God. And then I began to think I never heard Him in the first place.

During the days when doubt was trying to squeeze out hope, an old police injury plagued Kris for months and months, sometimes keeping him bedridden for days. I let doubt tell me God wasn't watching and that, while we were happy for Kris's career as an electrician, it was just another temporary and futile attempt at a career other than law enforcement. I let doubt tell me we could never be as happy as we were when we were blue. And Lord knows that isn't going to happen ever again. Stress and worry jumped right back into the mix as if they never left. And I knew all this would lead right back to my pit.

So, I stepped back from working in the nursery. I help here and there, but I returned to the services, up front with my husband. Right where I needed to be. And like I'd never left at all, the feeling, the urge to write came over me, and I saw my daddy. Not "saw" as in hallucinate. But a mental picture. Almost like those flashbacks I have. I don't want to "pretty up" the experience, so this is exactly what I scribbled in Kris's notebook while everyone else was singing.

> "Today I saw you. Like the flashbacks I have so often
> that push their way into my head, so my mind's eye is
> filled with your injuries and brokenness; your autopsy
> report coming to life. But today the flashback was

different. While singing, I saw you running in front of me. And when you turned toward me, I saw you at 20-25 years old, with long, hippie hair, smiling and laughing. I saw your motorcycle behind you. Not as the pieces that sit in my garage and some wrecking yard, three years later...I saw it whole, and new and shiny.

"So many times, I have sat in church and wondered at everyone dancing and jumping. Throwing their hands up and understanding the Holy Ghost has filled them, and I have wondered, 'Why not me?' And now I sit here with this beautiful image, but I'm not overcome with any manic joy or urge to shout. A brief doubt answers, 'Because I'm not faithful, I don't really believe.'

"But a calm sensation tells me God is speaking peace to me. Finally, I see. In those moments of still that always came after falling into my own pit, He has come to me and spoken to me in a language I haven't recognized. And while its different than the language He may speak to the dancers and shouters, it is utterly perfect to me—my love language."

I know God enjoys praise and worship and there are parts of the Bible that speak of dancing. But for now, in my brand-new baby faith, I hope my praising Him in the peace and serenity that I allow myself to feel, and the smile I have as I look toward the cross, and the tears I let flow, speak to how tremendously grateful I am and how much I am in awe of how perfectly designed the whole of things are. And I keep on walking, tripping occasionally, sometimes down for the count, but never out of the game. With His help, I get back up and try to keep walking, because that's what we are designed to do.

Some cynics will ask, "And what has that gotten me?"

Man, I wish I could say we were:

> completely restored, and
> Kris had his name back, and
> I never struggle with PTSD and depression, and
> the corrupt police department had to pay us a million
> dollars for libel, and
> now we sit on a hundred acres in the country, and
> we will never have to work again.

But that is not the way of the world, and we have many, so many more, lessons to learn.

One day I struggled with intrusive thoughts on my way to work. All triggered by some minor inconvenience and a sharp word from Kris. (I gave a much sharper word back, Reader.) Feeling ashamed, I felt those needling thoughts searching for a foothold. I braced myself, wondering which memory my head full of ghosts would dredge up. I felt fear rise in my chest.

One of my oldest defense mechanisms against these feelings is anger. I put on some heavy rock music and turned up the volume to drown my thoughts. I could feel my defenses start to go up and I realized the old armor I have used so many times is not good enough anymore. I was about to walk into a classroom of students with my walls up.

My old armor is cold and calculated. How would my students react to this? Kids tend to be much more perceptive than adults. They can tell when we aren't our best. Kids that may have had a rough time at home were about to walk into my classroom where they would feel my cold steeliness.

I knew what I needed to do. I needed to turn off the heavy metal. I needed to pray. Reader, for all my book writing and churchgoing, I hate to admit, I liked the way my old anger and cold armor felt. But I also know it's full of cracks and it's the sort of armor any enemy loves. It's a roadmap to my weaknesses. I was nearly at school when I finally relented and put on a spiritual song. Not a happy go-lucky song, Reader. I needed a warrior spiritual song to fight this day. I didn't necessarily need a moving symphony about God's love. I needed a "kick-a** and take names" song, worthy of the Lion. (Forgive me, Reader, the cursing is something I am still working on, this wild mouth of mine is a hard one to tame.)

And then I prayed. I prayed for the fortitude to turn from my anger-armor to put on the armor of God. I prayed for strength. When I got to school, I met another teacher on my team, and I prayed with her. I prayed for our students. With that, my day was turned around. I let Jesus take control of my thoughts and He vanquished all anger and fear. I felt stronger despite not having my walls up. I tell you all this, Reader, to admit I still struggle, and I still have days that are hard. But now, I have hope. I may not have full retribution for all my struggles and trials, but I have hope and I have treasure stored in heaven.

And despite it all, we are so blessed:

> I have found fulfillment in teaching.
> I have hope that my new district is the final one.
> Kris, who has struggled so long with back injuries, now has a job he loves, he can take pride in, and that doesn't leave him bedridden for days at time.
> We both leave for work and return home at nearly the same time.
> We have time for our babies and for each other.
> We have time for church and for play.
> We are making headway into our debts.

We have comfort knowing that:

> Every day brings us closer to God.
> Our contentment in the simplest things is just as beautiful and fulfilling as if we had everything we asked Him for before.

We are blessed with a life where:

> I can come home to my babies and not worry about tracking in blood and guts.
>
> I don't worry about getting another phone call from my police husband.

Evil and hurt are a little more removed.

Perfection is not measured by never missing the old way of life, nor by how much money we have, but where perfection is peace and gratitude in the face of all things.

Life is more beautiful than if we had won every battle against the world and continued working shifts and going through the motions spiritually, holding on to some self-righteous belief that we were good because we were "law enforcement."

We are children of God, first, foremost, and it is right.

So believe me, Reader, God wants us to walk in faith.

> He gave us an instruction manual.
> He gave us a Church for learning and enrichment.
> He gave us family within the body to lean on.

Not every lesson will be clear, not every hurdle will be effortless. What good is triumph without the trial? It's not that He wants us to hurt or struggle. But there is so much more to be gained when we work through problems. That is the difference between knowledge and wisdom. Knowledge can be gained by being told information. Wisdom is gained through experience.

Strengthened in Fellowship

Since Revival, I have grown to realize that going to church and hearing sermons takes fellowship. In today's world, it's easy to watch any pastor, any sermon, any church, and any worship, sitting in bed with a bag of chips. But sitting there in isolation without fellowship doesn't breed the dedication and the drive to make it a habit. At least not for me. Without the camaraderie, the mentorship, the shared struggles, I would also eventually stop watching those sermons in bed. That is not to say that I place my faith in church itself, or in the people. I began to, and God gently corrected me as He so often does.

After completing the manuscript for this book, Kris fell ill with a terrible bout of ulcerative colitis. It was so bad he ended up in the hospital for several days. We stopped going to church. We were both too tired. And the longer we didn't go, the easier it became to miss. I felt let down that my brothers and sisters didn't notice our absence until I started reaching out almost a month later. I began to feel the same isolation and disappointment I felt when our police family turned their backs. After speaking with a couple of different friends and mentors, I realized that the only place to put my faith is in God or Jesus.

"It is better to take refuge in the Lord
than to trust in humans."
-PSALM 118:8

"Trust in the Lord with all your heart and
lean not on your own understanding."
-PROVERBS 3:5

Church is critical for fellowship, but people are fickle, and we all get caught up in our own lives. I was placing too much burden on my brothers and sisters and not enough into Jesus' hands. So I came to the revelation that being part of the church takes patience and forgiveness, introspection and understanding. We must always take a moment to reflect and not let our emotions get the better of us. We must always place our full trust in God.

So go to church. Fellowship with other believers. Hear a sermon. Read the book. Develop those habits that turn into passions and keep vigilant over your walk. Feed your faith. Nourish your resilience and build your stamina.

**For every step you take in faith,
God will cross eons.**

VALIDATION

I am a constant seeker of approval. I need to hear it. I am also a perfectionist, afraid of making a mistake. Writing this book has been filled with ups and downs and doubts and fears. It's no easy thing to lay bare our story. Our mistakes. Our journey. I know backlash will come. There will be those who judge us. I know that for all my faith and my grit, it will still hurt when people call Kris a deadbeat, a dirty cop, and me a complicit, selfish woman with a flair for drama. It will hurt most when people say I am delusional for my beliefs.

But my scientific brain has considered the facts, looked at the so-called coincidences, and the holes in "logical, earthly" explanations can only be filled with God. My place in this world, my purpose for life can only mean there is an intelligent design to our stories, our journeys, our very being. I am not a bundle of tissue and cells that belongs to the Earth. I belong to my Father. I know this because I am marked.

"And you also were included in Christ when you heard the message of truth, the gospel of your salvation. When you believed, you were marked in him with a seal, the promised Holy Spirit."

-EPHESIANS 1:13

The Fingerprint of God

The funny thing about fingerprints is that we teach people they are so fragile when left on surfaces. Any little thing like pressure, weather, debris, can ruin it...erase it. But, truthfully, Reader, some fingerprints last a lifetime. I have a dear friend who did a study on letters written by her grandmother. She was able to find fingerprints on these letters more than 30 years later. How much more permanent is the fingerprint of God? I am marked, sealed. Others will know me by this.

I am validated in this life knowing I cannot erase this mark. Much like my own fingerprints, they are permanent. The pattern does not change. I cannot remove them wholly. The marks and injuries I sustain will eventually be replaced by new cells, or if deep enough, make my prints that much more unique and identifiable. I struggle with the fear of disappointing Him, but I know that I am not big enough to remove His seal. I use the analogy of a fingerprint; the Bible uses a door or gate.

"I am the gate, whoever enters by me will be saved."

-JOHN 10:9

"What he opens, no one can shut. And
what he shuts no one can open."
-REVELATION 3:7

But what about all the bad things? What about Kris losing his boys? Losing his good name? What about the trial, the illnesses, the burdens, the loss? What about my daddy? For so many years, I looked up and I hated my situations and circumstances, and I was so angry that God did these things to me. It has taken me a long time to recognize what is of God and what isn't. God did not do these things to us. I'm not a hundred percent sure the Devil was behind it all either. Humanity can do bad all by itself. God says that no weapon formed against us will prosper. He never said it wouldn't form.

Sometimes we might disagree with God on what prospering is … I mean, Kris and I did lose a whole way of life and went through some very dark times. But we are still together, we are safe, and we are happy. It took a long time, but not so long as others have endured.

So did all the hurts and evils prosper? No. In the scheme of things, over a life, those tribulations did not "ruin" us as I once thought. I don't look at the world as being any rosier than it has ever been. I know that more struggles will come. I know that war is never far. I also know those battles have already been won. I know that pain will fade, and enemies grow tired. I know that luck is fickle, and I have a Rock. I know that life sprouts amongst the ruins.

My perspective has changed a lot over the last year. And maybe that's all we ever really need is a perspective change. To look at things with different eyes. To persevere and find how strong we are and how weak those battles are. To hear with different ears and find that we are being spoken to and that God is still with us.

Every day I am spoken to. I have been given signs and scriptures to live by. I don't reach for conclusions. I wasn't trained that way. Trust me Reader, the simplest solution is the truest. And when I pray for understanding, it is given. Not always in the manner I expect and not always the answer I want, but it is given. I find my validation every day and the comfort of it makes this life so much more joyous. The knowledge that I cannot ever be lost makes every journey worth embarking on. The knowledge that where I fail, He won't, makes every risk worth taking. Including this one. Writing this book, following through on what I've been asked. It is worth writing because He asked me. It is worth writing, because even in my failures, I have learned and grown and found validation in my life.

Even in our failures, we should find a validation of purpose. Even if it is just to learn lessons from these mistakes. We all have purpose.

You are not alone.

EPILOGUE

*"The light shines in the darkness, and
the darkness has not overcome it."*

-JOHN 1:5

The last thing to pass on to you, Reader, is one that is difficult for me. I have always taken pride in getting things done. In my accomplishments. In proving myself. Even from a very young age, I was dead set on proving anyone wrong who doubted me. Proving to Daddy I could ride after my horse, Dollar, stepped on me and broke two of my toes. Proving I was tough. Proving people wrong when they doubted me. Medaling at every meet in the hurdles and sprint relay my Junior and Senior years after a Coach told me I was too slow as a freshman. I'm not afraid of the long game. Enduring surgery after surgery to bear children. Sticking it out when things got dark with my husband. I take pride in my ability to prove myself. And pride is my downfall.

As I said in the beginning, hindsight is 20/20, and I realize there are times I barely survived because my pride got in the way. I insisted on pushing God aside, like an angry toddler trying to learn and gain their independence. How much easier would those times have been if I had leaned on Him? Even today, I don't always think to take everything to Him. I can lie to myself and pretend I don't believe He gets involved in the little things. But He has proven that statement wrong so many times. Time and again He has shown just as much attention to a minor bump in the road as He has to our major roadblocks in life.

The real problem is pride. "I can do it. I can fix it. I can handle it. I can overcome it." But the reality is, there has never been a time in my life when I didn't have His light. In the darkest moments, in the hopeless times, His light never went out. From the moment, even as a young girl, when I didn't quite "feel" the baptism, I had a light inside. Even when I turned away, I had already invited the light to come inside. The darkness never overcame it.

No matter how I ignored Him or how I thought I lost Him, He was there.

I took pride in this independence and toughness, not realizing that all along, I was being held high. I was on Daddy's lap, and it really felt like me driving. I was on my Father's shoulders, and I really thought it was me flying. For every trial, every heartbreak, every downpour, the light flickered, and it may have sputtered with my failure to keep it lit, but He was always there to ensure it stayed lit. A flame where there was no fuel, no oxygen, no way to sustain it. The light shone in the face of impossibility.

So, my last request, Reader, is to trust and to humble yourself. If you don't believe, humble yourself to the possibility that there is something else out there. A bigger purpose to life than just some cosmic accident. If you believe but don't have faith, humble yourself to the possibility that nothing is coincidence, thus the reason you are reading this book.

If you are angry, hurt, lost, humbly ask for help. If you are a prodigal son or daughter, thinking you have been forgotten, as I have felt so many times, through the trial, through the loss, look down, Reader. On whose shoulders do you stand? Because if you are alive, if you are breathing, that light is shining. And the darkness has not overcome it.

I hope you all laugh and smile and love, because we are all a part of the greatest story ever told. Just remember that our stories don't always have the happy endings we expect or hope for. Change your perspective to understand that everything that happens in this life is not an end. Our lives are a collection of stories that will all end the same. An ending that doesn't change, despite a bad chapter or two. The ending was already written. It is signed and sealed with a cross when we accept Jesus as our Savior. Have the strength and stamina to see each chapter through, regardless of the outcome. Because, in the end, the real end, we are all one family under an amazing Father who will call us home.

Your friend,

Amy

> *"Arise and shine for your light has come."*
> -Isaiah 60:1

TRIBUTE TO
MY DADDY

Daddy,

I hope you see the cover of this book and know I am not walking away from you. You are always with me. Everyday. Every minute.

I am walking away from the wreck. From the field. I spent a long time there. I lived in that mess of mud and metal for a very long time. I drive that road every week and I cannot continue to see it as anything more than your jumping off place. You didn't die in that field...you just jumped into eternity. But, if I had never walked away from the wreck, I would spend my life picturing it. I would have to drive the long way around to Mama's.

So, now that I have walked away and bared my soul, I can see it as the place where you were made whole. A place where you got all the answers to all your questions. A place where the night witnessed a fantastical blaze of glory fitting to the man who lived every day to its fullest. Not an ending, just a "to be continued." And while I am so sad that I am not part of that next story, I know that someday I will be.

You always told us that we would remember things. Those times you took us fishing, took us hunting, taught us to ride and work. And you were so right. I am so very blessed to have all those stories. So, I will weave them all together, a tapestry for Gemma and Gage, and I'll leave the ends undone until my story crosses yours again.

I hope you understand me spilling my guts, the family secrets, and the things we never told others. It's just something I have to do. Although, I know I will never be as great a storyteller as you, I hope I did you proud, and I can't wait to hear your story from this oh so long, but oh so brief, time apart.

I love you a bushel and peck.

Love,
Big

This is the last text my daddy, Dennis Jones, sent to his best friend the night he died:

> "You will tell my children one day that I died living life to the fullest, admiring my children, hopelessly in love with my wife, and afraid of God. And if my wife finds another man, I will rise again. Don't forget."

Dear Reader,

I hope you made it this far without any regrets for taking part in this journey.

As I finish, I realize there are so many more stories I want to tell, mostly about Daddy and what an incredible man he is.

About how the kid voted "Most Friendly" in high school grew up to be the toughest most badass man I've ever met.

About how he never met a stranger. One time he saw Ray Wylie Hubbard eating supper before a concert and asked him to play a song that night for him. During the concert, Ray Wylie Hubbard asked Daddy to stand and said to the crowd: "This man here requested a song. By the looks of him, I'd better do it."

But the most important story is about Jesus, and what an incredible gift it is that I can say, "What an incredible man my daddy IS," not was. Because of His sacrifice, Daddy IS still with me, a little apart, but never gone.

I hope you all laugh and smile and love, because we are all a part of the greatest story ever told. We are all one family under an amazing Father.

ABOUT THE AUTHOR

Amy Jones Neville was raised in the small town of Leonard, Texas. She has a Bachelor of Science in Forensic Science with minors in Biology and Chemistry. Amy served as a crime scene investigator from 2009-2019 and has a knack for spotting irregularities and coincidences amidst a forest of details. She now teaches high school science, including Forensics. Amy still applies her scientific lens to the world and tries to remain impartial when relating her experiences.

Amy and her husband, Kris, have 2 children, Gemma and Gage and reside in north Texas. The family enjoys their church events, hunting and being outdoors together. They have an affinity for all creatures great and small. Their pet family includes 2 dogs, a cat, a ball python, a rabbit, three leopard geckos and three tortoises, all rescues.

To contact Amy for speaking engagements, email her at amyjonesneville@gmail.com

NOTES

Part I: In the Beginning | The Rise

1   Ray Wylie Hubbard, *Conversation with the Devil*, 1999, Produced by Lloyd Maines & Ray Wylie Hubbard

2   John 1:5

Part II: Revival | The Enemy

3   John 1:5

Part III: Revelation | God's Voice

4   Ray Wiley Hubbard, "Conversation with the Devil," 1999, Produced by Lloyd Maines & Ray Wylie Hubbard

Made in the USA
Columbia, SC
10 July 2022